66
WAYS
GOD
LOVES YOU

Experience God's Love for You in Every Book of the Bible

Jennifer Rothschild

THOMAS NELSON
Since 1798

66 Ways God Loves You

© 2016 by Jennifer Rothschild

Published in Nashville, Tennessee, by Thomas Nelson. Thomas Nelson is a registered trademark of HarperCollins Christian Publishing, Inc.

Interior design by Mallory Collins

Thomas Nelson titles may be purchased in bulk for educational, business, fund-raising, or sales promotional use. For information, please e-mail SpecialMarkets@ThomasNelson.com.

Unless otherwise noted, Scripture quotations are taken from the Holy Bible, New International Version®, NIV®. Copyright © 1973, 1978, 1984, 2011 by Biblica, Inc.™ Used by permission of Zondervan. All rights reserved worldwide. www.zondervan.com. The "NIV"and "New International Version" are trademarks registered in the United States Patent and Trademark Office by Biblica, Inc.™

Scripture quotations marked ESV are taken from the ESV® Bible (The Holy Bible, English Standard Version®), copyright © 2001 by Crossway, a publishing ministry of Good News Publishers. Used by permission. All rights reserved.

Scripture quotations marked HCSB are taken from the Holman Christian Standard Bible®, copyright © 1999, 2000, 2002, 2003, 2009 by Holman Bible Publishers. Used by permission. HCSB® is a federally registered trademark of Holman Bible Publishers.

Scripture quotations marked KJV are from the Holy Bible, King James Version (public domain).

Scripture quotations marked MEV are taken from The Holy Bible, Modern English Version. Copyright © 2014 by Military Bible Association. Published and distributed by Charisma House.

Scripture quotations marked NASB are taken from the New American Standard Bible®, Copyright © 1960, 1962, 1963, 1968, 1971, 1972, 1973, 1975, 1977, 1995 by The Lockman Foundation. Used by permission. (www.Lockman.org).

Scripture quotations marked NKJV are taken from the New King James Version®. © 1982 by Thomas Nelson. Used by permission. All rights reserved.

Scripture quotations marked NLT are taken from the *Holy Bible*, New Living Translation. © 1996, 2004, 2007, 2013 by Tyndale House Foundation. Used by permission of Tyndale House Publishers, Inc., Carol Stream, Illinois 60188. All rights reserved.

ISBN-13: 978-0-7180-8770-8

Printed in China

18 19 20 21 22 GRI 8 7 6 5 4

Contents

CONTENTS

CONTENTS

Introduction

When I was eight years old, Grandma Sarah gave me a red leather bible. I carried it to church every Sunday, and I tried to read it even though the King James Version was way over my head as a third grader! But I loved my Bible. I loved the smell of the leather! I loved the sound the pages made as they turned beneath my fingers. I loved what I read—that God loved me—third grade me—with an everlasting love. Deep down, I knew there was something holy, something "other" about it. Something deep within me knew that just like the glue on the binding held its pages together, the truth in its pages would somehow hold me together too.

And it did.

When I turned fifteen, my world fell apart. I could no longer read the words in my red leather Bible because I couldn't see them. I became blind due to a retinal disease, and I could no longer read it. But the truth in its pages did hold me together—and its truth still does.

Now, as a grown-up blind woman, I use other

versions of the Bible along with the King James and I no longer finger through those thin, oniony pages—I listen to the Bible on audio and through apps on my computer and phone instead.

But no matter how I experience the Bible, it always has the same effect on me. One profound, unavoidable, irreducible, soul-quaking effect—I feel the love of God.

I want that for you too. God deeply loves you—He loves you with an everlasting love.

So God tells you in sixty-six ways . . . in each and every book of the Bible.

From Genesis to Revelation, you'll see how much you matter to God. As you read through the history and poetry in the Old Testament books, you'll be reminded that God knows you and sees you and loves you no matter what. As you experience the Gospels and letters in the New Testament, you'll feel how His love challenges and changes you.

My prayer for you is that you, too, will feel the profound, unavoidable, irreducible, soul-quaking effect of His love as you experience it in sixty-six ways.

JENNIFER ROTHSCHILD

March 2016

In Genesis
God Fashions Me
with His Hands

In the beginning God created. He said, "Let there be light" and there was light! He spoke it. He commanded it. He just said it and it was! He called into existence that which had never existed before.

Every word became our world. Stars and planets. Shimmering sunshine and fierce lightning. Mountains and oceans. Forests and animals. Birds and sea creatures. Towering trees and tiny flowers. God's voice initiated all creation. All except man. God did not speak man into being because man was different—man was loved. "The LORD God formed man from the dust of the ground and breathed into his nostrils the breath of life, and man became a living being" (Genesis 2:7 MEV). Our beautiful Creator stooped down and got the dirt of this earth on His hands to give us life. God used His hands, His touch, to craft us—the crowning jewel of all His handiwork. And after He formed man, He gently fashioned a

woman from the rib of Adam with those same hands. He lovingly shaped her to reflect the beauty of her Creator.

God could have spoken you and me into existence, too. But He chose that we—His beloved ones—would bear His fingerprints. His touch separates us from all created things. It honors us above all other created beings. His touch on our lives constantly reminds us that we are loved.

You aren't just the result of God's verbal command to some genetic matter. You are the result of the loving Hand of God that reached all the way from heaven to touch you and make you His own. And He is still reaching and still touching you. "God saw all that he had made, and it was very good" (Genesis 1:31). Can you see His fingerprints on your life? Thank God today for His loving touch, and ask Him to keep creating you to be the beautiful person He loves.

In Exodus
God Delivers
Me from Slavery

For more than four hundred years, the Israelites were slaves in Egypt. They were stuck, mistreated, and without rights, yet they were still God's people. He had not forgotten His beloved. Suddenly, in flames of love and fury, God spoke through a burning bush. "I have indeed seen the misery of my people in Egypt. I have heard them crying out. . . . So I have come down to rescue them" (Exodus 3:7–8). The Israelites wondered for centuries if God really loved them, and one day His love set a bush ablaze before Moses' eyes. And God's love set about rescuing His people. When the people were finally free, Moses sang, "In your unfailing love you will lead the people you have redeemed. In your strength you will guide them to your holy dwelling" (15:13).

Just as God delivered His people from the slavery of Egypt, He delivers you from whatever you are powerless to rescue yourself from. Because He has "set His love upon you" (Deuteronomy

7:7 KJV), He sets you free from the slavery of sin, insecurity, fear, and despair. He frees you to trust and follow Him into all the promises He has for you. Just as He said, "the cry of the Israelites has reached me, and I have seen the way the Egyptians are oppressing them" (Exodus 3:9), your cry for freedom has reached His heart too. He loves you, and He sees what you are going through. He knows what oppresses you, what depresses you, and from what you long to gain your freedom.

God's love rescues you! He can break the chains that keep you stuck in your Egypt. Ask Him to set you free today. You can trust His mighty, loving Hand to keep rescuing you and setting you free.

Commemorate this day, the day you came out of Egypt . . . because the Lord brought you out of it with a mighty hand. (13:3)

In Leviticus
God Grants Me
Access to Him

God loves you so much that He made a way for you to come to Him, know Him, and love Him. Yet true access to God demands a true understanding of Him, so God gave us Leviticus.

In Leviticus, God drew His people to know Him as He really is—pure and holy. He loved them too much to let them settle for a false god or a reduction of His holy character. God devised ways for His people to experience a holy relationship with Him—He gave them rules. The rules weren't a way to earn a relationship with Him. Rather, they were to guide the Israelites' relationship with Him. The rules kept their hearts focused on the true God and brought them security.

Just as a loving parent provides protective boundaries for her child, God provides rules for us, His children. But it isn't following the rules and staying in the boundaries that win God's favor; we already have His favor because we have His Son, Jesus.

Because God loves us, He lets us know what is expected. He gives us rules and boundaries so we can approach Him with faith and purity. He gives us His commandments, and "His commands are not burdensome" (1 John 5:3).

Because God loves you, He makes a way for you to come to Him through His Son Jesus, and He also gives you rules so you can enjoy your best life with Him. But don't let the rules trip you up—God uses them as guard rails to keep you walking with and toward Him. And don't let any rules from God become a substitute for a relationship with God. "This is what the LORD has commanded you to do, so that the glory of the LORD may appear to you" (Leviticus 9:6).

God wants you to come to Him, know Him, and be with Him because He loves you. He promises, "I will walk among you and be your God, and you will be my people" (Leviticus 26:12). Thank Him today for being a loving Father who values you enough to show you the way to walk with Him, and ask Him to draw you to purity in your relationship with Him.

In Numbers
God Shelters Me
in Cities of Refuge

When God divvied up the promised land among the tribes of His chosen people, He gave the Levites forty-eight towns. Six of those towns were chosen by God to be cities of refuge. These cities were to be places where anyone could flee for safety if they were wrongly accused or running for their life.

God told Moses, "Select some towns to be your cities of refuge, to which a person who has killed someone accidentally may flee. They will be places of refuge from the avenger, so that anyone accused of murder may not die before they stand trial before the assembly" (Numbers 35:11–12). In other words, even though these were Hebrew cities, their gates were open to anyone who needed their safety. "Israelites and . . . foreigners living among them" (35:15) could find shelter there.

Cities of refuge are a picture of God's loving shelter for all of us. God made a place for us when

we were needy and accused by hiding us safely in His unconditional love and forgiveness. Just as the cities of refuge invited all into their gates, so God does the same for us.

We all need a city of refuge—a safe place where we know we are protected and welcome. God's unconditional love has become our city of refuge. When we run to Him, He welcomes us in, defends our honor, protects us, and preserves our lives.

If you need a refuge, Jesus says, "The one who comes to Me I will by no means cast out" (John 6:37 NKJV). He will be the wall that surrounds you, the shelter that protects you. Run to Him for refuge today. Ask Him to shelter you in His unconditional, unfailing, unending love. "God is our refuge and strength, a helper who is always found in times of trouble. Therefore we will not be afraid" (Psalm 46:1–2 HCSB).

In Deuteronomy
God Keeps His
Covenant of Love to
Me and to a Thousand
Generations

He has declared that he will set you in praise, fame and honor high above all the nations he has made and that you will be a people holy to the LORD your God, as he promised" (Deuteronomy 26:19).

That's what Moses told Israel—it was a reminder of how much their promise-keeping God loved them. And this was *after* Israel had blown it by bowing to the golden calf. It was forty years later, and God gave the law a second time to the Israelites because the generation before had failed so miserably that they didn't make it out of the wilderness. Yet in an unimaginable display of faithful love, God gave the law to a new generation, knowing that they, too, would fail Him and forget His promises.

The people needed reminding of God's promise of love, just as we all do from time to time. Especially when we've blown it. When we fail God, we wonder if God will fail to love us still.

But God's love for you is a promise—a covenant. The same God who promised His love to Israel is the God who loves you, and His love never fails (1 Corinthians 13:8). It spans millennia.

God's faithful love gave Israel the second law, and it gives you second chances. His covenant of love is a promise that He will give you His Word and remind you of His Word when you forget it. God's faithful love means He will never reject you even when you blow it. He will find you worthy of His affection even when you fail.

"Know therefore that the Lord your God is God; he is the faithful God, keeping his covenant of love to a thousand generations of those who love him and keep his commandments" (Deuteronomy 7:9). Thank God today for being a generous giver of second chances, and praise Him for never giving up on you.

In Joshua
God Gives Me
Divine Purpose

In the book of Joshua, Moses had died and Joshua was now leading God's people. The wilderness wanderings were over, and the time had come to take the land God promised His people. But the Israelites' enemy had gotten there first and had put up the No Vacancy signs. Though God had promised the land to the Israelites, the Canaanites already possessed it.

But when God gives a promise, He gives us a purpose. God told Joshua to take the promised land for God's people. "Be strong and of good courage, for to this people you shall divide as an inheritance the land which I swore to their fathers to give them" (Joshua 1:6 NKJV).

God probably hasn't given you the divine purpose of kicking Canaanites out of the promised land, but He has given you great purpose. We all have had times and seasons when we felt aimless, but even in those seasons you are not without purpose. God gives you the highest calling—the divine purpose of your life. He has called you "to love the LORD your God, to walk in all His ways, to keep His commandments, to hold fast to Him, and to serve Him with all your heart and with all your soul" (22:5 NKJV).

God loves you too much to leave you without purpose. He has called you to love Him, to walk with Him, and to follow His Word straight into the promised land. God doesn't leave you aimless, without direction or strength. Just as He had a divine purpose for Joshua, He has a divine purpose for you—a great purpose.

Jesus said, "Whoever practices and teaches these commands will be called great in the kingdom of heaven" (Matthew 5:19). You have been given the magnificent purpose of living out the words of Jesus and sharing them with others. Thank God for giving you the highest purpose—knowing and loving Him and making Him known. "The LORD . . . is with you wherever you go" (Joshua 1:9 NKJV), so be strong and courageous today as you live out your divine purpose.

In Judges
God Shows Mercy
in Spite of My
Repeated Failures

The book of Judges is my story. It's your story even though it was first ancient Israel's story. God rescued His people, and for a while they were grateful. Then they ran after other things, forgetting what God had done for them. So God, in His severe mercy, let them taste the fruit of all their choices. Life was bitter.

They came to their senses and cried out to God for deliverance. God rescued them, but unfortunately, the cycle started all over again—faith followed by failure.

Like each of our stories, however, the book of Judges isn't ultimately about our failures; it's about God's faithful love. Our human frailty and failure serve as a spotlight on God's unstoppable love for us.

"I led you up from Egypt and brought you to the land of which I swore to your fathers; and I said, 'I will never break My covenant

with you. And you shall make no covenant with the inhabitants of this land; you shall tear down their altars.' But you have not obeyed My voice. Why have you done this?" (Judges 2:1–2 NKJV)

God loves us enough to keep His covenant with us even when we don't keep our end of the deal. He loves us enough to confront us, let us fail and flounder, and even let us forget Him. But He loves us too much to let us go.

God meets your repeated failures with His radical faithfulness! His mercy is new every morning, and His faithfulness is great—greater than your worst mistake, deeper than your greatest regret, and bigger than any blunder.

"In those days there was no king in Israel; everyone did whatever he wanted" (Judges 17:6 HCSB). But today, you do have a King who is ready to extend mercy to you. The King of kings loves you and gives you mercy and faithful love. He does it when you least deserve or expect it. Keep walking toward God's faithful love, and you will find it. Lean into the mercy of God today, and find that His mercy is so much bigger than any mess you may have made.

In Ruth My
Kinsman-Redeemer
Grafts Me into
His Family

Everybody wants to belong. But Ruth and her mother-in-law, Naomi, were outsiders. Both were widows, alone in a foreign land. Naomi had buried a husband and two sons in Moab. So she did all she knew to do—she tucked away her grief, packed her bags, and went back home to Bethlehem. Ruth, from Moab, gave up her family and homeland to go with Naomi.

But when they arrived, neither Naomi nor Ruth could own the property that had belonged to their husbands. They were dependent on Naomi's male relatives to take care of them. So the men gathered at the city gate, and the nearest kinsman was offered the right to redeem the property—including all its liabilities. "I want to redeem it" the kinsman responded (Ruth 4:4 HCSB). But when he heard that Ruth went with the deal, he changed his mind.

Ruth: first widowed, now rejected by a man who she hoped would take care of her. She longed to belong.

Then Boaz stepped into her life. "I will also acquire Ruth the Moabitess, Mahlon's widow, as my wife" (Ruth 4:10 HCSB).

Boaz fulfilled Ruth's longing with belonging.

We, like Ruth, long to belong. And as Boaz made Ruth his family, God chooses us to be His family. We "who once were not a people . . . are now the people of God" (1 Peter 2:10 NKJV). As Boaz became Ruth's kinsman-redeemer, Jesus has become our Redeemer!

That means Jesus takes all your liabilities and makes them His own. His love makes you family. Thank God today for making you His own, and remember that even if you feel alone or like an outsider, you are loved by your Redeemer and you belong to Him forever.

Respond to God's beautiful love for you by telling Him today, "Where you go I will go, and where you stay I will stay" (Ruth 1:16).

In 1 Samuel
God Anoints Me
with His Spirit

When God went looking for a king, He chose the least likely of Jesse's sons: the youngest, the shepherd boy. Then He sent Samuel the prophet to find him. Samuel sought David out.

"Then Samuel took the horn of oil and anointed him in the midst of his brothers; and the Spirit of the Lord came mightily upon David from that day forward" (1 Samuel 16:13 NASB).

God anointed David with His own Spirit. He chose David for a purpose so much bigger than what he could have imagined as he tended sheep. God gave the young shepherd His Spirit to accomplish His calling.

To be anointed means to be selected and appointed. You may feel like the least likely to be chosen or singled out for divine purpose, but you, too, are anointed with God's Spirit. Just as David didn't achieve his own anointing, you don't achieve yours either; you receive it from God when you receive Christ.

When you trust Jesus as your Savior, His Spirit lives in you—you are anointed with His Spirit. First John 2:20 says, "You have an anointing from the Holy One and . . . you know the truth."

And Jesus said His Spirit, "the Spirit of truth[,] . . . lives with you and will be in you" (John 14:17). God loves you so much that He wants not only to be with you, but in you—that is why He anoints you with His Spirit.

As He did for King David, the Spirit of the Lord will be "mightily" upon you every day of your life. And His Holy Spirit continually anoints you with purpose and strength. Though you may sometimes feel like an overlooked shepherd boy, God sees you and chooses to anoint you with His Spirit for a purpose that is so much bigger than your perception of yourself and your abilities.

Ask God to refresh you with His Spirit today so you can walk in your anointing.

In 2 Samuel
God Builds a
Home for Me

In the book of 2 Samuel, David, the former shepherd, had become the king. He ruled over Israel from his palace built of cedar. But his heart was grieved because God had no proper house. "The ark of God remains in a tent," he lamented (2 Samuel 7:2). So David planned to build a house for God—until God reversed the whole thing. Instead of David building a home for God, God said, "I will provide a place for my people Israel and will plant them so that they can have a home of their own and no longer be disturbed" (7:10).

Isn't that just like our loving God? We seek to build a home for Him, and He instead builds a home for us! God gives us a home in His heart and in His family. He makes us part of His kingdom just because He loves us.

God was building a forever home through David. That forever home not only included the forty-year reign of King David, but every believer to come. David's reign began a royal house, a forever home, that eventually would be ruled by King Jesus, and that will include you and me too.

Sometimes we can feel alone, insecure, not sure that we really belong. But God has proven that you are part of His best building project ever! "You are a chosen race, a royal priesthood, a holy nation, a people for God's own possession" (1 Peter 2:9 NASB).

He has made a place for you in His kingdom and built a home for you in His heart.

Thank God today for making a home for you in His kingdom and in His heart. Show Him you love Him by making room in your heart for Him too.

In 1 Kings
God Remains
Faithful to Me

God's love is faithful even when we're unfaithful. And we have all been unfaithful. We've broken promises, failing to follow through on what we said we would do. Many of our days have started with great faith—and ended in great failure.

We aren't alone. The Bible tells us that "Solomon loved the LORD and followed all the decrees of his father, David, except that Solomon, too, offered sacrifices and burned incense [to idols] at the local places of worship" (1 Kings 3:3 NLT).

David's son Solomon had become king, and he was considered the wisest man who had ever lived (4:31). But that wisdom didn't keep him on a path walking faithfully with God. He was faithful and unfaithful, steadfast and unsteady, human and, uh, human! We humans are consistently inconsistent.

But even though Solomon had been unfaithful, our faithful God refused to take the entire

kingdom away from him, "for the sake of my servant David, the one whom I chose and who obeyed my commands" (11:34 NLT).

God doesn't measure His faithfulness on the scale of your behavior or track record. God is faithful to you even when you are faithless. And He does this for Jesus' sake. When you are in Christ, Christ is in you, and God cannot be unfaithful to you without turning His back on Himself! As Paul wrote, thousands of years after Solomon, "If we are faithless, He remains faithful, for He cannot deny Himself" (2 Timothy 2:13 NASB).

So, no matter what you have done or how far you have wandered, God's faithfulness is waiting to forgive, restore, refresh, and renew your relationship with Him. Shift your focus today from your failures to God's faithfulness. You will discover unfailing love and unconditional forgiveness.

In 2 Kings
God Shows Me
Loving Patience

God shows His love through action. Sometimes, though, He shows His deepest love for you by not acting. Have you ever looked at our world and asked, "Why doesn't God do something?" The answer just might be, "Because of His patience." God just keeps giving us chances—because He loves us.

Throughout 2 Kings, Israel and Judah made the same mistakes over and over again. They had some good kings and some bad kings; they made some good choices and some bad choices. But God was patient. When a leader turned to the Lord, God powerfully guided. When the king followed other gods, Yahweh let the kingdom reap the painful results. Through it all God was patiently working out His plan to save and redeem the people He loved.

The Bible tells us that ancient Israel "did evil things, provoking the LORD. They served idols, although the LORD had told them, 'You must not do this'" (2 Kings 17:11–12 HCSB). Sometimes our world seems just like them.

It may seem that God isn't acting as quickly as He should when it comes to the evil or injustice in our world, but "the Lord isn't really being slow about his promise, as some people think. No, he is being patient for your sake. He does not want anyone to be destroyed, but wants everyone to repent" (2 Peter 3:9 NLT). His apparent inactivity is not a sign that he lacks compassion but, rather, an indication of his deep love—and incredible patience toward us.

God could strike out against His people; instead, he patiently strives with them. He endures our sinfulness with patience. This is where we see His love in action; in "the riches of his kindness, forbearance and patience" (Romans 2:4). God is unwilling to give up on us or give us up to our waywardness. His patience demonstrates His extreme compassion toward us.

Thank God today for His patience toward you, and ask Him to grant you patience toward others who may be stuck in patterns of sin and unfaithfulness.

In 1 Chronicles
God Grants
Me Success

God's love has crowned you with success that has nothing to do with your achievements. You may hesitate to label yourself "successful." But if you have walked very long with the Lord, you can look at your history and be amazed at what God has done in you, through you, or even in spite of you!

As a shepherd boy, David could have never imagined what God would do with his life. But as king, he looked back and said to God, "Who am I, Lord God, and what is my family, that you have brought me this far?" (1 Chronicles 17:16). David saw his own success and was astonished.

Sometimes we measure our success by what we've done or where we came from or who our family is. And when we do, we can think that if we've not done much with our life or if our past is marked by big failures or a dysfunctional family history, we just aren't a success.

But the God who loves you has given you

success that has nothing to do with your performance, your past, or your pedigree.

You may not be the king of a nation or the CEO of a company; you may not even be able to keep your house tidy or your children in matching socks! You may have a failed marriage or be unemployed. But like David, you have been granted success by your loving God because He has brought you so far. When you can look deeply into your own soul and humbly ask, "Who am I . . . that you have brought me this far?" you are beginning to grasp the kind of success you have been given.

When David considered what God had done in his life, he said, "You . . . have looked on me as though I were the most exalted of men" (17:17). David got it. He understood that success isn't something you achieve; success is believing the reality of who God is and what He says about you.

Ask God today, "Who am I that You have brought me this far?" And, then listen for His voice. He will reassure you of His love and remind you of all He has done in your life.

In 2 Chronicles
God Makes My
Prayer Powerful

Finally, the long-awaited temple was finished: beautiful, bejeweled, and beyond anything the Israelites had ever seen. On dedication day, King Solomon "stood before the altar of the Lord in front of the entire community of Israel, and he lifted his hands in prayer" (2 Chronicles 6:12 NLT).

But even as King Solomon prayed thousands of years ago in a splendid temple in a foreign land for people you've never even met, you were included in that prayer: "In the future," the king said, "foreigners who do not belong to your people Israel will hear of you. They will come from distant lands when they hear of your great name and your strong hand and your powerful arm. And when they pray toward this Temple, then hear from heaven where you live, and grant what they ask of you. In this way, all the people of the earth will come to know and fear you" (6:32–33 NLT).

There has never been a moment when you were not on God's mind and in His heart, and that's why you are in the king of Israel's prayer. But even more astounding is that Jesus, the King of the universe, prayed for you too. "I pray also for those who will believe in me through [the disciples'] message," He said (John 17:20).

"When Solomon finished praying, fire came down from heaven and consumed the burnt offering and the sacrifices, and the glory of the Lord filled the temple" (2 Chronicles 7:1). God loved Solomon and heard his prayer. God loves you and hears your prayer too.

The fire of His love falls when you pray, and His glory fills you—His living, breathing, beautiful temple (1 Corinthians 6:19). So pray, not because you feel powerful, but because your loving God makes your prayer full of power!

In Ezra God's
Persistent Love
Restores Me

Do you ever feel as though you're living among the ruins of what you once hoped life could be? Dreams fade, relationships fail, and people fall. Sometimes we look at the landscape of our lives and there's only rubble of what once was and the unfinished foundation of what we tried to build.

Ezra knew those feelings, and so did the people of God who had just returned home from seventy years of captivity by the Babylonians. They returned holding their breath—holding out hope of restored grandeur—but instead, they found ruins. Their temple and the city of Jerusalem had been destroyed. So the returnees worked for ten whole years to get the temple foundation laid. Yet, even when it was finished, the older people wept because it was so disappointing compared to Solomon's temple (Ezra 3:12).

Even though God was restoring all things for His people, the restoration was slow and hard and even discouraging. But eventually, the temple was rebuilt and the people's hope was restored. "He has granted us new life to rebuild the house of our God and repair its ruins, and he has given us a wall of protection in Judah and Jerusalem," they said (9:9).

God restores us through His persistent love even when we feel the sting of profound loss. Like Ezra and the Israelites, though, we may find that our restoration project can be slow and hard and even discouraging at times.

We can look back, like the oldest Israelites, and weep because our dreams have not come true as quickly as we had hoped or in the way we had hoped. But God is not done with us; His love is persistent even when we feel impatient.

God's love will build you up in your spirit as you trust Him to restore your broken places. He will grant you "new life to rebuild" what is broken, and His love is strong enough to "repair its ruins."

Ask God to help you see your life today the way He sees it. Focus on how He is rebuilding, restoring, and making all things new. Thank Him for being the Master Builder, who restores lost hope and rebuilds broken souls.

In Nehemiah
God Gives Me
Tools to Rebuild
All That Is Broken

In this life, brokenness is inevitable—but it doesn't have to be permanent. Just ask Nehemiah.

Though Nehemiah and his people were in captivity in Babylon, Nehemiah himself had a cushy job in the king's palace (Nehemiah 1:11). Life was good.

Then word came that God's people were suffering in Jerusalem. The walls were broken down. The people lacked protection (1:3).

God called Nehemiah to return and lead the rebuilding. But rebuilding requires tools. God not only gave Nehemiah the tools he needed but also made Nehemiah into the tool He would use to rebuild the walls and gates of Jerusalem.

You, too, are a tool in the hand of the Master Designer. Even with brokenness in your life, He can still use you to accomplish His purposes, but He also supplies you with what you need to accomplish the job set out for you. He can use

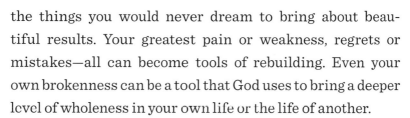

the things you would never dream to bring about beautiful results. Your greatest pain or weakness, regrets or mistakes—all can become tools of rebuilding. Even your own brokenness can be a tool that God uses to bring a deeper level of wholeness in your own life or the life of another.

Nehemiah and his crew rebuilt the wall of Jerusalem in a miraculous fifty-two days. And when the enemies of God saw, "they were frightened and humiliated. They realized this work had been done with the help of our God" (6:16 NLT).

God has a beautiful plan for your life. He wants to rebuild in and through you so all will see what God has worked. The design will be greater than you would have imagined, and God will supply every tool you need to accomplish it. Be on the lookout for the tools God is providing. Don't resist what He may be using, even if the work is hard. And make yourself available to be that tool that He can use to repair and restore what is broken in the people you encounter and the places you go today.

In Esther God
Crowns Me with
Worth and Makes
Me Royalty

She was just an orphan girl, raised by her cousin. They were Jews in Persia. Her people had been taken captive more than a century before. An orphaned foreigner was about as far from royalty as you could get.

But God raises the lowly and crowns them with honor. His love took an unknown orphan named Hadassah and turned her into a queen named Esther. Here is her story.

This orphan from an outcast minority was ripped from the only home she knew and thrust into a harem. Terrified. Insecure. Unsure. But Esther, we are told, "had a lovely figure and was beautiful," and she "won the favor of everyone who saw her," so she moved quickly to "the best place in the harem" (Esther 2:7, 15, 9).

Esther caught the king's eye and eventually stole His heart. "She won his favor and approval more than any of the other virgins. So he set a royal crown on her head and made her queen" (2:17).

Pulled from obscurity into a place of honor, Esther is still remembered today. Every spring Jews celebrate Purim and read Esther's story. Children playact her life, and every little girl wants to play Esther. God not only made her royalty, but He also used her to save her people and honored Esther across the ages.

God makes you royalty too. As Esther won the king's favor, you have won the King of king's favor! You have caught His eye and stolen His heart! The King is "enthralled by your beauty" (Psalm 45:11).

God's love elevates you from the state of an orphan to the status of honored monarch. No matter who you are or where you've been, even if you don't feel worthy of being called God's beloved, God crowns you with worth. You may not believe that you're worth His effort, but God thinks you *are* worth it. So bow your head in humility and feel the love of God place a crown on your head. God sees you. God loves you. God wants you.

As you look into the mirror today, a queen will be looking back at you. Open the eyes of your heart to see who you really are and how much you are loved.

In Job God
Sustains Me
in Suffering

Possibly the oldest book in the Bible, the book of Job—every page of it—is stained by tears. It tells one of our oldest stories—we all suffer, and suffering hurts.

Job was a good guy, "blameless and upright; he feared God and shunned evil" (Job 1:1). Even so, Job lost his wealth, his children, and his health. On top of that, his wife scolded instead of supported him, and his friends lectured instead of loved him. Job sat in an ash heap, covered with sores, heartbroken and discouraged, and still said of God, "But he knows the way that I take; when he has tested me, I will come forth as gold" (23:10).

God loved Job, and God loves you. He doesn't allow suffering because He is displeased, disappointed, or punishing you. God allows the suffering that breaks His heart to accomplish in you what will eventually strengthen, cleanse, and beautify your own heart.

God didn't save Job from suffering; He sustained him through it. And God will do the same for you. The same God who "suspends the earth over nothing" (26:7) is the God who holds you when you feel your sorrow may crush you.

If you feel like Job, remember that God's love surrounds and sustains you. Nothing touches your life that has not first penetrated His heart and passed through His loving hand. Trust that "He performs wonders that cannot be fathomed, miracles that cannot be counted" (9:10). God can and will perform wonders and miracles in your life either by saving you from suffering or by sustaining you through it.

Often God chooses to love us through suffering because it moves us from just having a little information about God to a place of intimately knowing and depending on the God who loves us. Thank Him for using your suffering to help you see Him and His love for you more clearly. As Job said, "My ears had heard of you but now my eyes have seen you" (42:5).

In Psalms My
Good Shepherd
Draws Me Close
and Listens
for My Voice

Shepherds still travel with their flocks across the arid landscape of Israel today. And just like the shepherds of old, today's shepherds know their sheep. They know what scares them; they know when just one of the flock wanders off. They guide and protect them because they are theirs.

David called the Lord "our Shepherd" because we are God's sheep. "We are the people of His pasture, and the sheep of His hand" (Psalm 95:7 NKJV), he wrote. And just like sheep we, too, need a shepherd to guide us and protect us.

Without God's guidance, we wander and get caught in the thistles of life. If He doesn't lead us beside still waters, we will get spiritually dry and worn out. If He leaves us alone, the wolves of lies and evil will pounce on us and devour our faith and confidence.

God is the Good Shepherd—your Good Shepherd who draws you close and watches

over you. He invites you to lie down in green pastures; He refreshes your soul and guides you along the right paths. And even the darkness of the valley of the shadow of death doesn't have to frighten you because God doesn't ever leave you. "I will not be afraid," the Psalmist sang, "for you are close beside me (23:4 NLT).

Your Good Shepherd sees your tears and listens for your voice. Again, David cried, "You, LORD, hear the desire of the afflicted; you encourage them, and you listen to their cry" (10:17).

Let your Good Shepherd carry you today through the valleys or the victories. As you walk with Him, talk with Him. He knows you and loves you and hears you, and He wants His "goodness and love [to] follow [you] all the days of [your] life" (23:6).

In Proverbs
God Offers Me
Wisdom More
Precious Than Rubies

The God of the universe calls you His own, His beloved child. And your heavenly Father has riches and wealth at His disposal. He could give you anything because nothing is too hard or too big for Him.

God could show you that He loves you by lavishing you with luxury, moving you into a new house, getting you out of debt, and making you a billionaire. But when God expresses His love to His child, he does it by offering you something far more valuable than gold, something more priceless than any precious gemstone. He gives you wisdom. Why? Because wisdom will "prolong your life many years and bring you peace and prosperity" (Proverbs 3:2). "If you become wise, you will be the one to benefit" (9:12 NLT).

God could give you anything, but He chooses to give you wisdom. Wisdom is knowledge, with the spiritual insight to judge what really matters. And it is yours for the asking!

Just as God gave Solomon a wise and "discerning heart" (1 Kings 3:9) when he asked for it, God is leaning over the edge of heaven even now, listening for your request, just waiting to fill your heart with wisdom too. So if you lack wisdom, "ask of God, who gives to all liberally" (James 1:5).

God gives His most precious and valuable gifts to His children. That is ultimately why He gave you Jesus—and Jesus is the "wisdom of God" (1 Corinthians 1:24).

Thank God today for loving you so much that He only gives you the very best gifts—including that gift that is more precious than rubies.

> *Blessed is the one who finds wisdom,*
> *and the one who gets understanding,*
> *for the gain from her is better than gain from silver*
> *and her profit better than gold.*
> *She is more precious than jewels,*
> *and nothing you desire can compare with her.*
> *(Proverbs 3:13–15 ESV)*

In Ecclesiastes
God Gives
Meaning to
My Meaninglessness

When we seek the eternal God over temporary pleasure, we find the meaning we long for. Just ask the aged King Solomon.

The book of Ecclesiastes contains Solomon's reflections on his life as he sat on the back porch, watching the sun set and the shadow of death draw near. He'd had good days as a younger man. When the Temple was dedicated, he was wholeheartedly devoted to God. But over the years, his heart had become divided, and eventually it led to his kingdom being divided too. He surely shook his head remembering how he'd shifted from seeking God to seeking pleasure in everything the world offered. His self-indulgences had left him empty. It was all meaningless.

But Solomon's past also shimmered with admirable things, like success, fame, and wealth. He'd expected those kinds of things to bring him joy and meaning, but in his old age he said, "When I surveyed all that my hands had done

and what I had toiled to achieve, everything was meaningless, a chasing after the wind; nothing was gained under the sun" (Ecclesiastes 2:11).

You can have it all, but if you don't have God, it is meaningless. That's why God stepped into our history. He gave us meaning when He gave us Himself.

God loves you so much that He gives you something greater than stuff or success or sensations to fill the empty places in your heart. He fills your emptiness with His peace, purpose, and presence. And in doing so, He replaces your meaninglessness with meaning.

At the end, Solomon figured it out: "Here now is my final conclusion," he wrote: "Fear God and obey his commands, for this is everyone's duty" (12:13 NLT).

Meaning doesn't come when we get all we want; it comes when God becomes all we need. If we only seek happiness, we will find frustration. But if we seek God, we will find meaning. Seek Him today above all things and you will find that you have all you need.

You have meaning in your life when you have God in your life.

In Song of Songs
the Lover of My
Soul Draws Me
to Run After Him

The bride was shy and self-conscious. But the groom sang over her with delight. "O most beautiful among women," he intoned (Song of Songs 1:8 ESV). Solomon was in love, captivated by this woman, so he wrote a song, but not just any song, the Song of Songs. Solomon had written more than a thousand songs, but none better than the one he sang over the woman he loved.

In the Song of Songs, Solomon recorded the longing, the affection, the beauty as the lovers sang to each other during their weeklong wedding feast, which began their life together: "Behold, you are beautiful, my love; behold, you are beautiful" he sang to her (1:15 ESV).

"My beloved is mine and I am his," her heart sang in response (Song of Songs 2:16). The pure melody of his passionate love drew her to trust him and give herself fully to him.

God is the Lover of your soul who sings over you. Like Solomon, He sings, "You are altogether beautiful, my darling, beautiful in every way" (4:7 NLT). You can trust His lyric of love and give yourself fully to Him.

God loves you passionately, perfectly, and personally. He doesn't just want you as a believer or a follower. He wants you as His beloved. He loves you, and He draws you to Him so you will love Him back.

Sometimes we only think of devotion to God as duty. But God considers time spent with you as delight. He delights in you as does a master in his painting, a groom in his bride, or a mother in her newborn. That's why "[H]is banner over [you] is love" (2:4 NASB).

Rest beneath that banner today. You may feel shy or self-conscious, insecure or unworthy, but trust that God unconditionally loves you. He has placed you like a "seal over [His] heart" (8:6). You can trust that His love will never, ever let you go because "love is as strong as death, its jealousy unyielding as the grave. It burns like blazing fire, like a mighty flame" (8:6).

In Isaiah
God Reveals to
Me the Savior

True love knows your greatest need and does whatever it takes to meet that need. Your greatest need is a Savior. We need someone to take away our sins and make us clean and new. We can't meet our greatest need on our own, so the love of God set about meeting that need through His Son, Jesus. "My righteous servant will make it possible for many to be counted righteous, for he will bear all their sins" (Isaiah 53:11 NLT).

When God spells love, He spells it J-E-S-U-S. And seven hundred years before the infant Jesus was even laid in a manger by His scared, astonished young mother, God showed us who He would be.

God wanted you to know His Son. So He revealed that Jesus would be a branch from the root of David (11:1); a child called *God with us* and born of a virgin (7:14); a great light to the people who walk in darkness (9:2). Jesus—the ultimate expression of God's love for you—is the "Wonderful Counselor, Mighty God, Everlasting Father, Prince of Peace" (9:6).

It began in a cradle and led to the cross: God's love revealed, your greatest need met. God loves you too much to keep His most beautiful gift a secret. He offers you the gift of salvation that is in Christ alone. "Though your sins be as scarlet, they shall be white as snow; though they be red like crimson, they shall be as wool" (1:18 KJV). Thank God for His most profound revelation of love for you—Jesus. Ask Him to reveal the Savior to you fresh and new today. Take time to think about what God has saved you from by giving you Jesus, and then thank Him for His greatest gift.

"I will tell of the kindnesses of the LORD,
the deeds for which he is to be praised,
according to all the LORD has done for us." (63:7)

In Jeremiah
God Sees My
Tears and Gives
Me Hope

Sometimes we just need to cry, don't we? And who can understand that need better than one who felt it so deeply? The prophet Jeremiah is called the weeping prophet, and of all the people who walked the pages of the Old Testament, Jeremiah most resembles Jesus. The weeping prophet reminds us of our tenderhearted Savior, who is willing to be broken and weep for the people He loves.

It was so dark for God's people. They had hit rock bottom, and their nation was destroyed. They found themselves in a seven-decade exile in Babylon. They longed for home. They wept for what had been. In that time of destruction, Jeremiah preached the heartbreaking and heart-boosting truth that the nation would fall but that God's love would stand. "I have loved you, my people, with an everlasting love. With unfailing love I have drawn you to myself" (Jeremiah 31:3 NLT).

God saw His people's tears, and He sees yours. He promises you that even through the blur of sorrow, a light of hope shines brightly—no matter the destruction; no matter the loss.

For the people in Jeremiah's day, God gave them the hope of going home again. He assured, "A great company will return! Tears of joy will stream down their faces, and I will lead them home with great care. They will walk beside quiet streams and on smooth paths where they will not stumble" (31:8–9 NLT).

Even when tears fall, hope stands. God says to you, "For I know the plans I have for you . . . plans to prosper you and not to harm you, plans to give you hope and a future" (29:11).

The love of God shows up in your darkest moment as the light of hope. And hope turns even your tears of sorrow into tears of joy. So if you need to cry today, go ahead and let it out. Then lift your face to God and feel His love wipe away your tears and give you hope.

In Lamentations
God Grants Me
New Mercy
Every Morning

In the sixth century before Christ, every new morning the sun rose to reveal the same old broken dreams. Jerusalem was destroyed. Solomon's beautiful temple, which had stood for almost four hundred years, was rubble and ash. The Babylonians had trampled and plundered, leaving nothing but despair in their wake. When the Israelites woke to a new day, they felt the same old discouragement wash over them. They grieved; they cried out to God—they lamented.

We may not call it "lamentations" when we cry out with grief or sorrow, but that's what we're doing—lamenting. Some days, when morning dawns, we are just consumed with sorrow—overwhelmed with loss, and we lament because we are facing the same old discouragement.

But God meets your old discouragement with new mercy: "for his compassions never fail. They are new every morning" (Lamentations 3:22–23).

God doesn't want yesterday's trials to be your source of despair. He doesn't intend for yesterday's triumph to be your source of strength either. God gives you new mercy each day, and that new mercy will be your source of strength—the perfect portion you need to make it through whatever the day brings.

"Because of the Lord's great love we are not consumed [by sorrow]," says Lamentations 3:22. God is faithful to you just as He was to the Jews in Jerusalem. Nothing that happened to them could destroy God's steadfast, unfailing love or prevent His mercies from falling upon them like the noonday sun.

No matter what happened yesterday, and no matter what happens today, you will not be consumed. If you are weary and worn-out, count on God to give you new mercy for today. Like Jeremiah, say to your soul, "The Lord is my portion; therefore I will wait for him" (3:24).

In Ezekiel
God Brings Life
to My Dead Bones

Ezekiel was just a young man when he was uprooted and marched off to Babylon. For five years, he saw nothing but despair. But when he was thirty, a vision of God's glory captivated him, and everything changed. Ezekiel became a priest and prophet. God told him to speak into the lives of the despairing and defiant Israelites so they would know "a prophet has been among them" (Ezekiel 2:5). And they *needed* to hear from the Lord, because of the horrible way they felt: "Our bones are dried up and our hope is gone; we are cut off" (37:11).

So God took Ezekiel, the prophet and priest, to a valley of dry bones and asked him a faith question: "Son of man, can these bones live?" Ezekiel had the honesty to say, "Sovereign Lord . . . you alone know" (37:3).

Sometimes we look at the landscape of our lives and see only a valley of dry bones. We look at dead dreams, lifeless hopes, and ruined relationships, and with Ezekiel, we wonder, *Can these bones live? Can all this really come back to life? Can hope be resurrected? Can all the ruin in my life really be restored? Can God breathe life into these dry bones?* We all face times when everything seems dry and dead. We can only summon a weak, "Lord, You alone know the answer."

God does know the answer to the question your heart asks as you face your dry bones. God *is* the answer. His love resurrects what seems lost forever. His compassion mercifully breathes life back into what you think may be hopeless. And His promise to us today is, "I will put breath in you, and you will come to life. Then you will know that I am the Lord" (37:6).

Open your spiritual eyes today to see that God, and God alone, can turn your valley of dry bones into a wellspring of hope. Then ask Him to breathe new life into you.

In Daniel
God Joins Me
in the Fire

Sometimes God doesn't deliver us from the fiery trials we face. Instead, He delivers us *through* them. When He does, we experience His love through His presence.

Daniel's three friends were told to worship a statue of King Nebuchadnezzar or feel the flames of the king's fury and be thrown into a blazing furnace. They told the king they wouldn't bow and that, even if they were thrown into the fire, "the God whom we serve is able to save us" (Daniel 3:17 NLT).

The God who loves you is also able to save you from the fire you face, though His love may choose not to prevent your fire. Even so, His love will be present there. Sometimes we see God's love for us most clearly when He chooses to endure the sorrow with us, to feel the pain right there beside us.

The king had Daniel's three friends thrown in the furnace, but the king was shocked to "see four

men walking around in the fire, unbound and unharmed" (3:25). God Himself had joined them in the fire.

God will not let you walk through fire alone either. He joins you right there. If you feel the sting of fiery trials today, look right beside you. You will see that God is with you in whatever you face. He will be the same "fourth man" whom King Nebuchadnezzar saw when he looked into the furnace that day in ancient Babylon. He will not look like "a son of the gods" (3:25); He is the very Son of God!

Thank Him today for loving you enough to walk with you through whatever you face. If God hasn't prevented your suffering, look for His presence in your suffering. God may not save you from feeling the fire, but He will save you from enduring it alone. Trust Him to be with you today, for "no other god can save in this way" (3:29).

In Hosea
God Pursues Me
to Buy Me Back

We all want a love that won't let us down, but what happens when we let down the one we love? That could be the end of the love story, but Hosea shows that's when the real love story begins. Hosea the prophet married Gomer—a promiscuous woman. She was the least likely to be selected, but Hosea chose her. Then Gomer began chasing after other lovers. She left the husband who loved her and went from man to man—until she found herself standing on a slave block, auctioned to the highest bidder.

Hosea's heart was broken. He must have felt humiliated. But the Lord told him to "go and love your wife again, even though she commits adultery" (Hosea 3:1 NLT), so Hosea followed God's word and bought her back. He paid the price of a slave, but He didn't treat her as a slave. He brought her home and restored her to the position of a beloved wife.

Hosea and Gomer's love story is the story of

God's love for Israel, but it is also our love story. God loves you so much that He paid the ultimate price—Jesus—to buy you back from sin's slavery and to bring you home. Though we have broken God's heart as Gomer broke Hosea's, the Lover of our souls seeks not to punish us but to dress us in robes of purest white. He, like Hosea, says to each of us, "I will make you my wife forever, showing you righteousness and justice, unfailing love and compassion" (2:19 NLT).

You were not intended for chains; you were chosen to be a beloved bride, safe in the promise of God's love. Look in the mirror today and see Gomer looking back at you. She was the beloved—chosen, accepted, and loved—and so are you. Even if you've wandered away from God, He is pursuing you. Receive the unconditional love of God today.

In Joel
God Restores
the Years the
Locusts Have Eaten

They were everywhere: a relentless swarm of locusts had overwhelmed the nation of Judah. The insects destroyed everything—the gardens, the fields of grain, the vineyards, and the trees. It was so bad that Joel compared the hefty hoard of locusts to a marching human army and, with a broken heart, said that God was showing divine judgment against the nation because Judah had turned her back on God. In fact, He was using the angry insects to discipline His children. Love often shows up as discipline. And discipline isn't pleasant. But the same love that disciplines also restores. God said, "I will repay you for the years the locusts have eaten" (Joel 2:25).

All of us have places in our lives where the "locusts" have eaten—missed opportunities because of bad choices, mistakes made, and losses piled on. God often uses those hard places as His Fatherly hand to nudge us forward—to

teach us and train us. Sometimes the locusts in our lives—what we think is hurtful interference—are really God's loving intervention. God's gentle, and even not-so gentle, discipline makes space in our lives for the outpouring of God's Spirit (2:28–29).

Those locust times and places are not dead ends; they can become the path to greater blessing. As Paul put it thousands of years later, "In all things God works for the good of those who love him, who have been called according to his purpose" (Romans 8:28).

God may not replace what you have lost, but He will redeem what you have lost. Even your most agonizing loss—even your worst day—will be redeemed as God works it all together for good. Focus today not on the pain of discipline but on the promise of deliverance. Focus not on what you have lost, but on how God is using that loss to grant you greater blessing.

In Amos God
Protects Me When
I Feel Powerless

Because God loves people, He hates oppression. He hates anything that takes advantage of you. In Amos's day, the rich were ruthless and exploited the poor: the Lord Himself said of them, "They trample the heads of the poor on the dust of the ground and block the path of the needy" (Amos 2:7 HCSB).

God's perfect love turns into an angry flame against those who take advantage of the disadvantaged. Both Amos and God were furious toward those "who rob the poor and trample down the needy!" (8:4 NLT). There were people who cheated and strong-armed and exploited those who most needed a hand. They mixed in chaff with grain and rigged scales so they could charge more. And when they employed the poor, they didn't offer a fair wage. "Then you enslave poor people for one piece of silver or a pair of sandals," God accused (8:5–6).

Love does not overlook injustice. It will not

ignore the unprotected and underprivileged. God's justice will come for every oppression. But even more than that, God will restore far more than this life can take from us. "'The days are coming,' declares the LORD, 'when the reaper will be overtaken by the plowman and the planter by the one treading grapes'" (9:13). In other words, love will eventually bring a harvest of justice and blessing in your life that no oppressor can stop.

If you feel as if what you've planted in life has been trampled on or your efforts are uprooted before they can even have a chance to grow, trust that God's power is greater than the powerlessness you feel. Pray today, "Let justice roll on like a river, righteousness like a never-failing stream!" (5:24).

In Obadiah
God Stands
Up For Me

Bullies. Mean girls. We've all had to deal with them, and they come in many forms. Selfish family members destroy homes. Two-faced friends gossip. Sometimes we just need a big brother, a protector who will do something about it. In ancient Israel they called Him Yahweh Elohim. You know Him as "the Lord your God."

The Israelites were running for their lives. They needed help, so they asked their cousins—family who should have stepped up and stepped in. But the Edomites didn't fight for the Jews; they fought against them. They turned their backs on their cousins and turned them over to the enemy.

God would not overlook Edom's pride and betrayal: "'Because of the violence you did to your close relatives in Israel, you will be filled with shame and destroyed forever. When they were invaded, you stood aloof, refusing to help them. . . . You acted like one of Israel's enemies.

101

You should not have gloated when they exiled your relatives to distant lands. You should not have rejoiced when the people of Judah suffered such misfortune. You should not have spoken arrogantly in that terrible time of trouble'" (Obadiah vv. 10–12 NLT).

Sometimes, when the bullies attack, it just helps to realize that God knows and cares—He even gets mad about it! God isn't ignoring injustice just because He is allowing it. Justice will be done. God has your back. The book of Obadiah has only one small chapter, but with one big message: the God who loves you fights for you even when it feels everything is against you. If you feel the sting of being bullied or wish someone had stood up for you when you needed it most, look to God today. He is standing up for you and standing with you no matter what you face. And if you feel as though you may crumble, ask Jesus to stand up tall within you. He will. "You, O Lord, are a shield about me, my glory, and the lifter of my head" (Psalm 3:3 ESV).

In Jonah God
Uses Imperfect
Man to Fulfill
His Perfect Plan

God's love won't let us go even when we twist, tug, and try to run! Just ask Jonah, the most disobedient prophet ever. God called him to preach to Nineveh, but Jonah didn't want to. So he ran to the nearest seaport and booked passage on a ship heading the opposite direction. God had a perfect plan, but Jonah was an imperfect man.

Our human frailty can't mess up God's sovereignty though. On his way to Tarsus, a fierce storm came up, and Jonah went down into the ocean. That should have been the end of Jonah, but God's love would not let him go. For Jonah, mercy was a giant mackerel with a man-sized appetite!

From the belly of the fish Jonah said, "In my distress I called to the Lord, and he answered me. From deep in the realm of the dead I called for help, and you listened to my cry." (Jonah 2:1–2)

Even when we start to slip off the path God has lovingly planned for us, God never loses track of us. Not for an instant. He knew how and where to find Jonah, just as He knows how and where to find you and me when we veer from the perfect path God chooses for us. He swallows us up in His mercy when we are sinking in sin, just as He did for His reluctant prophet—whom God had the fish spit out on shore, to live to see another day.

God kept loving and using a man who did everything the opposite of God's command. He didn't give up on Jonah, and He won't give up on you either. God still accomplished his goal of saving the Ninevites in spite of the stubborn prophet. Jonah concluded, "Those who cling to worthless idols turn away from God's love for them. But I, with shouts of grateful praise, will sacrifice to you. What I have vowed I will make good. . . . Salvation comes from the LORD" (Jonah 2:8–9).

Thank your perfect God for His perfect ways and ask Him to use you in His plan today.

In Micah God
Invites Me to
Walk Humbly
with Him

Listen closely and you can hear it—an imaginary conversation between God and His people Israel. They wanted to know what, in our most private thoughts, we want to know too: "How much is enough?" and "Am I acceptable to You, God?"

Israel asked innocently enough, "With what shall I come before the LORD?" (Micah 6:6), but then escalated to the heights of hyperbole:

Will the Lord be pleased with thousands of rams, with ten thousand rivers of olive oil? Shall I offer my firstborn for my transgression, the fruit of my body for the sin of my soul? (6:7)

It was as if they were pleading, "Is that good enough? Is that the formula? Is *that* what You expect from us?"

Because God loved them, He gave them—and us—in one perfect statement what He expects. "He has shown you, O mortal, what is good. And

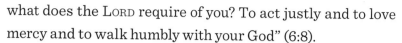
what does the LORD require of you? To act justly and to love mercy and to walk humbly with your God" (6:8).

Israel was focused on their "to do" list, when God was focused on their hearts. Loving, just people who walk humbly with Him is what God really wants.

Israel wanted a formula, and so do we—just tell us what to do. But God desires friendship over formulas, and that's why He invites us to walk humbly with Him. When we walk with God, more focused on His love than on our list, the natural outgrowth is just and loving actions. And that's what God desires because that is what brings us the most blessing.

More than a list of sacrifices performed for Him, God wants a life shared personally with Him. Accept His invitation to walk humbly with Him today.

In Nahum
God Gives Me
Refuge in Times
of Trouble

For Nahum, every day was a bad day. His people—who had once stood proud and strong—hung their heads under the weight of poverty and shame. They were stripped of their freedom; their dignity stolen. They had to pay exorbitant taxes to Assyria just to hold on to what little freedom they had. Nahum's prophet heart was heavy as he looked at the calendar that never changed. No quick turning of the page led to better days. He needed a refuge. His people needed a place to hide within long, bad days.

But tucked within the calendar of bad days was comfort from God—the Ancient of Days! The prophet found refuge in God's comfort that would come to His people: "The LORD is good," he cried, "a strong refuge when trouble comes. He is close to those who trust in him. . . . Look! A messenger is coming over the mountains with good news! He is bringing a message of peace" (Nahum 1:7, 15 NLT).

No matter what you see written on the calendar of your life—trouble, sorrow, or fear—God also writes refuge and comfort across every day. He takes care of and comforts His people. You need never fear. God has not forgotten you.

The Assyrians were eventually brought to their knees, and their "endless cruelty" came to an end (3:19). We can take comfort in the truth that God does eventually punish evil, and He never overlooks it when His children are mistreated.

Do you need His comfort today? Look to God's comfort to be your refuge in times of trouble. Better days are coming—the page will turn. Walking across the coming months and years on the calendar of your life are "the feet of [one] who bring[s] good news, who proclaim[s] peace" (Isaiah 52:7). Ask God to be your refuge today. Look for His peace to fill your day and be your comfort.

In Habakkuk
God Places My
Lowliness in
High Places

Life is full of low places—injustice and abandonment plummet us to the bottom of ourselves and leave us feeling down. Habakkuk found himself in some low places, so he went to and confronted God: "How long, O LORD, must I call for help? But you do not listen! . . . The law has become paralyzed, and there is no justice in the courts. The wicked far outnumber the righteous, so that justice has become perverted" (Habakkuk 1:2, 4 NLT).

When Habakkuk felt as if he were sinking in the quicksand of confusion and frustration, he climbed his watchtower, seeking an answer from God. But God gave him something better than an answer. He lifted Habakkuk's spirit and gave him perspective on suffering even when God wasn't preventing the suffering. In response, Habakkuk said, "Even though the fig trees have no blossoms, and there are no grapes on the vines; even though the olive crop fails, and the fields lie empty and

barren . . . yet I will rejoice in the LORD! I will be joyful in the God of my salvation!" (3:17–18 NLT). Habakkuk didn't rejoice because his problems changed; he rejoiced because his perspective changed. God lifted His lowly prophet to "tread on the heights" with Him (3:19).

And God will do that for you too. If you find yourself in a low place, do what Habakkuk did—go honestly to the Lord with your hurts or frustration. When you do, God will give you His perspective; He will lift your spirit to "tread on the heights."

Thank God for lifting your spirits when you are down and raising you up to see your problems from His perspective. Ask God today to help you see, like Habakkuk, that what you need most is not answers to your questions, but an encounter with Him. For God's presence is far more valuable than answers.

In Zephaniah
the Mighty God
Sings over Me
with Great Joy

Something about you inspires God to sing—to sing over you! He delights in you. God loves you as only a perfect Father can love a child—and it shows up in gladness and joy when He thinks of you. "The Lord your God is living among you. He is a mighty savior. He will take delight in you with gladness. With his love, he will calm all your fears. He will rejoice over you with joyful songs" (Zephaniah 3:17 NLT).

Many—maybe most of us—think that even if God loves us, He must not like us very much. We assume God just endures us, but He doesn't enjoy us. We wonder if He harbors secret resentment, or if He must be continually cross because of our sin. We worry that one day He will just stop singing, mid-song, and stomp off! But that is not God's heart toward you. This is:

> *"The Lord has taken away your punishment;*
> *he has turned back your enemy.*

The Lord, the King of Israel, is with you;
never again will you fear any harm." (3:15)

Hear the words of Zephaniah, a stern prophet, not shy about telling God's people to straighten up when they'd blown it. Yet Zephaniah insists that God delights in you. Far from shaking His fist or wagging His finger at you, God sings a lullaby at your bedside. His serenade of perfect love can calm any concern. He quiets the insecurity that you don't qualify for His love and settles that inner fear that you're just one mistake away from Him walking away.

The lyric of God's love song reminds you that God isn't disgusted with you; He delights in you. God doesn't just tolerate you; He celebrates you. Perhaps today, you need to tune in and hear His song. And then you can sing back to Him!

"Sing, Daughter Zion;
shout aloud, Israel!
Be glad and rejoice with all your heart,
Daughter Jerusalem!" (3:14)

In Haggai God
Himself Dwells
with Me and
Gives Me Peace

They were finally home. The Jewish people had been exiled in Babylon, but now they were in the land God promised them. They started to rebuild the Temple—but then got discouraged and distracted, so they quit.

God's dwelling place among them was the temple—and His temple lay desolate. Only God's presence among them could grant them courage and focus to follow through and press on toward the goal of finishing the rebuilding. His presence was the peace they needed. So they laid down their discouragement and picked up their hammers once again to work on God's house.

God assured them that "'the glory of this present house will be greater than the glory of the former house . . . And in this place I will grant peace,' declares the Lord Almighty" (Haggai 2:9).

God's peace is what we need most also. And we find His peace in His presence. God's presence can remove the clutter of fear and

discouragement. It makes a path of peace for us to walk when we need to press through discouragement and courageously trust and serve Him in whatever ways He calls us to. His presence assures us that we are not alone, forsaken, or abandoned.

The ragtag group in Haggai's day pressed through their discouragement to build a temple for God's presence to dwell with them. But five hundred years later, God presented the Prince of Peace Himself at that very temple: Immanuel—God with us (see Luke 2:22–40).

Because God loves you, He makes His dwelling with you and gives you peace. Jesus said, "In me you [will] have peace" (John 16:33). God in flesh came to live with you and with me. And because He came, we have peace. Peace is not the absence of discouragement; peace is the presence of God. Ask God to dwell with you today, and thank Him for His peace.

In Zechariah
God Assures Me
of His Coming

Throughout the pages of Zechariah, God whispers, *"Don't worry, child. Even if it feels like the world—your world—is a mess, your Messiah will come."* The love of God for you is fully proven in the Son of God, who has come for you. The prophet Zechariah foretold His coming: "Rejoice, O people of Zion! Shout in triumph, O people of Jerusalem! Look, your king is coming to you. He is righteous and victorious, yet he is humble, riding on a donkey—riding on a donkey's colt" (Zechariah 9:9 NLT).

Sometimes we feel unsure because the world seems to spin out of control. Injustice, violence, fear, and turmoil can make us want to look back to better days or cast our eyes down. But we can look forward to better days—to the best day ever! We can be assured that "the LORD will save his people on that day as a shepherd saves his flock. They will sparkle in his land like jewels in a crown" (9:16).

Just as the Jews looked forward to the coming of Messiah, a day will come when the Messiah comes again! On that day He will complete the promise: "a fountain will be opened to the house of David and the inhabitants of Jerusalem, to cleanse them from sin and impurity" (13:1).

Love promises us "that day" will come!

Jesus—the Messiah, the hope of all nations—will come! Just as He came into Jerusalem five hundred years after Zechariah made his prediction of a "king . . . riding on donkey's colt," He will come again on "a white horse," and He who sits upon it will be called "Faithful and True," and "on His robe and on His thigh He [will have] this name written: KING OF KINGS AND LORD OF LORDS" (Revelation 19:11, 16).

God promised a Messiah, and He sent Jesus. God promises that Jesus will return, and He will. Ask God to infuse you today with the hope and rejoicing of "that day" so you can feel the calm assurance that all you see right now is not all there is!

In Malachi God
Pours Out His
Blessing on Me

One of the ways we show we love someone is by giving gifts. Israel's entire relationship with God had always been built around that principle. God loved gifts from His people, and He poured gifts upon them. But by Malachi's time this gift exchange had lost some sincerity on the part of the Israelites. They held on to the form of loving God, but they had forgotten the reality. They went through the motions of worship, but their worship had become meaningless. Their hearts were ungrateful, and they skimped on what they gave to the Lord in worship.

Malachi declared: "The Lord of Heaven's Armies says to the priests: 'A son honors his father, and a servant respects his master. If I am your father and master, where are the honor and respect I deserve? You have shown contempt for my name!' But you ask, 'How have we ever shown contempt for your name?' You have shown contempt by offering defiled sacrifices on my

altar. Then you ask, 'How have we defiled the sacrifices?'" (Malachi 1:6–7 NLT). The people God loved so deeply were not only being stingy with their hearts toward God, but when challenged about it, they argued like teenagers.

God's response is surprising. Rather than punishing or berating them, God poured out blessings on them. He said over and over that for those who will come to Him with wholehearted love and devotion, He will "open the windows of heaven [and] pour out a blessing so great you won't have enough room to take it in!" (3:10 NLT).

God's blessing pours out of His heart of love for you. Even when you talk back like an ungrateful child, God holds back His anger and gives you kindness instead. "'I have always loved you,' says the LORD" (1:2 NLT).

So don't hold back your love for God. Open your heart to love Him without reservation, and as your heart is open, His love will pour over your life with unconditional acceptance.

In Matthew
God Puts On
Human Flesh Just to
Seek and Save Me

God's limitless love for us is so big—yet it fit in a tiny manger.

"This is how the birth of Jesus the Messiah came about: His mother Mary was pledged to be married to Joseph, but before they came together, she was found to be pregnant through the Holy Spirit" (Matthew 1:18).

Mary's baby boy was born in a manger in Bethlehem, and hope was born on earth. "All this took place to fulfill what the Lord had said through the prophet: 'The virgin will conceive and give birth to a son, and they will call him Immanuel'" (1:22–23). Jesus is Immanuel—God with us. God proved your value to Him once and for all through Immanuel.

Immanuel doesn't mean "us with God." Immanuel means God with us. God pursued you. He came to seek you and to save you. He became flesh to be "with us." He allowed Himself to be wrapped in swaddling clothes to be "with us." He walked solitary paths in dusty sandals, felt hunger and pain to be "with us." He rode the crest of tumultuous waves and tasted the salt of His own tears at Lazarus's tomb—because to weather storms and endure loss are part of being "with us." His hands touched lepers, and His back carried our cross so He could be with us.

The God who loves you is with you. He came to be with you because we need a "God with us." We are unable to be with Him . . . without Him. He initiates companionship. He draws us to Himself. He pursues us tenderly.

Many world religions have gods who demand "us with god." Work. Strive. Please. Clean up. Try harder. Be better. Pursue. Then, just maybe, that god will be with us. Christianity has the one true God, who seeks to be with us and makes it possible for us to be with Him. Any requirements for us to be with God were met by Jesus. Through Christ, we are reconciled with God (Colossians 1:19–22).

The Son of God is the Son of Man, who came to be with you, to seek you, and to save you. "For the Son of Man is come to save that which was lost," Matthew tells us (18:11 NASB). Receive and respond to His loving pursuit today, and find the compassion and companionship you long for.

In Mark
God Stills the
Storm in My Soul

Dusk was settling over Galilee. Jesus had been teaching the crowds all day, but as twilight dappled the horizon, He and His disciples boarded a boat to cross the lake. Jesus fell asleep in the back of the boat, and "a fierce storm came up. High waves were breaking in the boat, and it began to fill with water. . . . The disciples woke [Jesus], shouting, 'Teacher, don't you care that we're going to drown?'" (Mark 4:37–38 NLT).

Sometimes the winds of life toss us, and we feel as if we will surely drown beneath fierce waves of stress, illness, or disappointment. And like the disciples, we can wonder if God cares that "we're going to drown." We long for God to just make it stop, to calm the storm.

There is no storm more powerful than your God. And He does care when you feel you may drown beneath the heartache of it all. His love can calm your heart even if His will chooses not to calm the storm. Sometimes He lets storms

remain to teach you something in the waves or build up your strength at the oars. And sometimes the very tumult you think may drown you is what God is using to cleanse you and carry you to a better place of deeper trust.

But sometimes God simply speaks peace, and the storm stills. "Silence! Be still!" Jesus said when His disciples woke Him up. He spoke to the raging storm, and "suddenly the wind stopped, and there was a great calm" (4:39 NLT).

God speaks peace to you today. And His peace will "guard your hearts and your minds in Christ Jesus" (Philippians 4:7). So if the winds of life toss you today, trust God's peace to ground you. If the waves of fear, doubt, anxiety, or stress threaten to wash over you and take you under, hold tight to Him, for He is in the boat with you.

In Luke the
Good Samaritan
Sees Me When
I'm Broken and
Comes to My Aid

The Samaritan in Luke's story was just another guy traveling—just like the priest and the Levite. They were all busy, on a schedule, and had places to go. But then, they saw a man who had been "attacked by robbers" (Luke 10:30). He was beaten up, left for dead, helpless, and hopeless on the side of the road. The priest and the Levite both "passed by on the other side" (10:31, 32), but the Samaritan crossed the bridge of prejudice, and "he took pity on him. He went to him and bandaged his wounds" (10: 33–34). The Samaritan gave of his time and money and risked his own safety and comfort to help the one who couldn't help himself.

God's love is our Good Samaritan when we are broken, needy, and can't help ourselves. When we've been beaten up by life, God's kindness wipes away our tears and bandages our broken spirits. When circumstances leave us feeling left-for-dead, God's love gives us life—and not just plain survival kind of life; He gives us abundant life! (John 10:10). When we've been abandoned, sidelined, overlooked, and forgotten, God's love sees us, comes to us, and scoops us up into His Heart.

We are all like that broken man on the side of the road—we are the ones who need God, need healing, and need help.

So, it's okay if you feel as though you are stuck and can't even pull yourself up by your own bootstraps. You don't need to. God's love comes to you, surrounding you and lifting your eyes to see better days. David wrote, "You, O Lord, are a shield about me, my glory, and the lifter of my head" (Psalm 3:3 ESV). Ask Him to pick you up and minister to your soul's deepest broken places. He will because He loves you.

In John
God Gives Me
Everlasting Life

For years Jesus loved the unlovables. He laughed with His disciples and listened to the pleas of the helpless and hurting. He lavished grace and forgiveness on all who opened their hearts to Him. He lived among us, "and we beheld His glory, the glory as of the only begotten of the Father, full of grace and truth" (John 1:14 NKJV).

Then it all came to a horrible, beautiful end. Jesus, the most loving person who ever lived, was alone in a garden, praying, asking God if there was any other way. But He knew. He knew there was no other way because He was The Way. Just as He told Thomas, "I am the way and the truth and the life. No one comes to the Father except through me" (14:6).

So He laid down His life for us. He hung on a cross and held the weight of our sin in His nail-pierced hands—whether we're religious or rebellious; humble or haughty; skeptical or

sincere. It was for each of us that Jesus died. It was for you that Jesus died.

You are the reason God grew a tree that eventually became a cross.

You are so valuable to Him that He is "not willing that any should perish but that all should come to repentance" (2 Peter 3:9 NKJV).

If you wonder just how much God really loves you, look to that horrible, beautiful cross where Jesus stretched out His arms as if to say, "This much . . . this is how much I love you."

The message of the Cross is that God will go to any length to save you, endure any pain to bring you peace, and experience any loss to rescue you. "For God so loved the world that He gave His only begotten Son, that whoever believes in Him should not perish but have everlasting life" (John 3:16 NKJV).

No one will ever love you more or better than Jesus. Let the shadow of the Cross fall upon you today, reminding you that you are loved—deep, wide, and forever!

In Acts
God's Spirit
Comes to
Live in Me

They had seen their Master die on a cruel Roman cross. One had tried to protect Him from arrest in the Garden of Gethsemane, some had fallen asleep while He prayed, and one had denied even knowing Him. Yet He had risen, and they'd seen Him again. Now they clung to each other and to His last words to them: "Do not leave Jerusalem until the Father sends you the gift he promised, as I told you before" (Acts 1:4 NLT).

The Gift God promised was His Spirit.

While Jesus was still walking the dusty roads of ancient Palestine, teaching and healing and loving and ministering, "the Spirit had not yet been given, because Jesus had not yet entered into his glory" (John 7:39 NLT). God's people didn't need the Holy Spirit with them because they had Christ Himself among them. But when Jesus had to leave them, even then they would not be left alone.

"When the day of Pentecost came, they were all together in one place," when suddenly, a fresh wind came from heaven and "filled the whole house where they were sitting" (Acts 2:1–2). That fresh wind demonstrated the gift of the Holy Spirit, whom Jesus had promised.

After the resurrection of Jesus, the Holy Spirit came to live in the hearts of believers, guiding and empowering them from within.

The Holy Spirit is God's love gift to you. When you trust Christ, He comes to live in you too, just as He did in those first followers. He empowers you from within also. He is a Counselor, an Advocate, a Helper, a representative of Christ, a Teacher, and the One who reminds you of truth.

God has not left you alone. His Holy Spirit is with you. And His Spirit counsels you when you are confused. He helps you when you are weak. He comforts you when you are sad, and He reminds you of truth when lies bombard you.

Listen for the Holy Spirit's voice today, for He has not left you "as orphans"; He has "come to you" (John 14:18). Follow His counsel and receive His comfort.

In Romans
God Works All
Things Together
for My Good

Nothing is wasted in your life. Nothing is a dead end. Nothing is totally futile, fatal, or fruitless. Nothing is worth nothing because God coordinates everything to create something good.

For "in all things God works for the good of those who love him, who have been called according to his purpose" (Romans 8:28).

God is the Master Potter, who never stops molding and shaping and creating and crafting good in our lives. He loves us and reaches down into the dirt of our lives—what we think is utter defeat or hopeless—and turns what we view as worthless into something priceless. He sees us as worth His time and His touch. Sometimes we feel as though our lives are a mess. But God does not see us that way. The stuff that you think may be just too messy, too ugly, too far gone is the very stuff God can use to create something beautiful.

The sorrow that hurts you? God can fashion it into faith that sustains you.

The sin you're ashamed of? God can use it to create beautiful humility.

The failures you regret? God can turn them into wisdom.

The grief that shattered your heart? God can craft that into unshakable faith.

The missed opportunities? God can use those to make you reflect His grace.

The loss you never expected? God can mold that into strength you can't explain.

God is using even the worst things in your life to create the best for you, His beloved child. He won't take His Hand off your life, because He has a divine design in mind for you.

God specializes in making old things new, turning scarlet sins into spotless snow, and transforming ashes into beauty. Trust Him with your burdens and your failings and your disappointments today and be encouraged! The God who loves you has got this! And "if God is for us, who can be against us?" (8:31).

In 1 Corinthians
God Teaches Me
the Way of Love

A little more than half a century after Jesus' death and resurrection, the apostle Paul founded a church in the city of Corinth, Greece. After he left the church, he heard some disturbing news. Some prickly characters had occupied the church at Corinth—folks filled with pride and who were bickering with one another. Some were immoral. Others were suing each other in court. They fought over food sacrificed to idols and were at each other's throats over worship. The Corinthians didn't know how to love one another! So, Paul put pen to paper to correct them, sometimes severely but always in love. He wrote, "I am not writing these things to shame you, but to warn you as my beloved children" (1 Corinthians 4:14 NLT). He loved them even though they weren't living the love they'd been given.

We are God's beloved too, and sometimes we don't live the love we've been given either. But God doesn't shame us; rather, He shows us the way to love by demonstrating it.

He says to you, His beloved, "[My kind of] love is patient and kind. Love is not jealous or boastful or proud or rude. It does not demand its own way. It is not irritable, and it keeps no record of being wronged. It does not rejoice about injustice but rejoices whenever the truth wins out. Love never gives up, never loses faith, is always hopeful, and endures through every circumstance" (13:4–7 NLT).

God teaches you the way of love by loving you well. He loves you with patience and kindness. He loves you by never giving up or walking out on you. God loves you perfectly because He is love.

God's love turns ordinary individuals like us with all sorts of differences into one family, diverse but dedicated to each other. It overcomes division and overlooks differences. It never demands uniformity but always brings unity.

God teaches you the way of love because He loves you deeply. He shows you the way of love so you will walk the path of love, giving to others what you have received from Him. So, "beloved, let us love one another, for love is of God" (1 John 4:7 NKJV).

In 2 Corinthians
God Comforts Me

Sometimes life can feel like one long winter. Loneliness haunts us, and grief leaves us barren and cold. But then the love of God rushes in like an April breeze of comfort, touching the deepest aches of our souls. God's comfort penetrates every fear and sorrow with the truth that we will be okay because God sustains us.

Paul knew that comfort. He wrote to his brothers and sisters in Corinth a second time, and this time, he bared his soul. The parchment was probably stained with tears, for his heart was so tender toward this church, where he had invested eighteen months of his life. Nowhere did Paul tell of his personal sufferings as in this letter, and he didn't do it to lament his suffering, but to lift up God's comfort. "All praise to God, the Father of our Lord Jesus Christ. God is our merciful Father and the source of all comfort. He comforts us in all our troubles so that we can comfort others. When they are troubled, we will

be able to give them the same comfort God has given us" (2 Corinthians 1:3–4 NLT).

God is your source of ultimate comfort too. He comforts you because He is your merciful Father, who cares deeply when you hurt. He sees your tears, hears your cry, and feels your pain.

Life is messy. Nothing can prevent the suffering that comes with life on planet Earth. But nothing can compare to the comfort God gives His children either. He says to you, "As a mother comforts her child, so will I comfort you" (Isaiah 66:13).

We experience God's love as He comforts us, and we express God's love as we comfort others with "the same comfort God has given us" (2 Corinthians 1:4 NLT). If grief or sorrow has left you cold and achy, find someone who needs to feel the warmth of comfort today. As you give comfort, you will feel the comfort of God blanket all your despair with His love and hope.

In Galatians
God Sets Me Free

Freedom rings from every book and every page of Scripture. But nowhere do the liberty bells peal more beautifully and clearly than in the book of Galatians. "It is for freedom that Christ has set us free," Paul wrote (Galatians 5:1). God's love has set you free from condemnation and confusion, free from the curse of sin, and free from the lie that you need to do something extra to be accepted by God.

And this freedom costs us nothing because it cost Jesus everything. God loves you so much that He purchased your freedom once and for all on the Cross. When Christ died and rose again, the final payment for your forever freedom was paid in full. You don't owe a penny or a penalty. You are no longer a slave to the sin that threatened to take you down. "We receive God's promise of freedom only by believing in Jesus Christ" (3:22 NLT). God has set you free through His Son, Jesus, and "if the Son sets you free, you [are] free indeed" (John 8:36).

You may feel stuck today in a habit or a mind-set. You may feel as if you are a slave to your past or to others' opinions. You may look at your life and still see the shadow of some chains that once shackled you to defeat or discouragement. But a bell is ringing in your spirit. It is the song of freedom stirring in your soul. It is what Paul rang for the believers in Galatia—you are free.

"Stand firm, then, and do not let yourselves be burdened again by a yoke of slavery" (Galatians 5:1). The God who set you free wants you to stay free—free to follow Him and walk in His love.

There is no chain, no shackle, stronger than God's love for you. And His love has set you free, so let go of any chain you may think is still yours and pick up the bell of freedom instead.

Ring it loud and long! Let it resonate in your spirit today, "for the law of the Spirit of life has set you free in Christ Jesus" (Romans 8:2 ESV).

In Ephesians
God Lavishes
Me with Grace

Grace is God's gift to you because you are a precious gift to Him. Grace is a smile from God that we didn't expect, forgiving words from Him that we didn't earn, and a welcoming hug that we didn't deserve. Grace doesn't show up when we're good or walk away when we're bad. It doesn't have a list of demands or a litany of desires. Grace forgives the guilty and covers the unworthy. Grace was standing up for us even when our faces were turned from God.

God lavishes us with His grace not because we deserve it, but because His love determined it. And that is the nature of grace; it is undeserved and unearned.

When we could have languished in our sin, God lavished us with grace instead. "For it is by *grace* you have been saved, through faith—and this is not from yourselves, it is the gift of God" (Ephesians 2:8, emphasis added). Grace gives us a tiny glimpse of "how wide and long and high

and deep is the love of Christ" (3:18) for us. And grace helps us "know this love that surpasses knowledge—that you may be filled to the measure of all the fullness of God" (3:19).

Before God designed mountain ranges, crafted raindrops, and dug His hands deep in the dirt of Eden to form man, "God decided in advance to adopt us into his own family by bringing us to himself through Jesus Christ. This is what he wanted to do, and it gave him great pleasure" (1:4–5 NLT).

Before God made the decision to create the world, he made another decision: to love you and "bring you to Himself through Jesus." The grace of Jesus is the bridge that brings you to God and makes a place for you in God's heart. You are saved by grace, sustained by grace, and satisfied, in the deepest part of your soul, by grace and grace alone. Receive His welcoming hug, His unexpected smile, and let His forgiving words wash over you. He longs to lavish you with His grace, so linger in His presence today and feel His unexplainable favor.

In Philippians
God Gives
Me Joy

Joy is a seed God plants in the hearts of His children so the sweet assurance of His presence will blossom in our lives. It is a fruit of His Spirit in us. It is peace dancing, a calm delight, an inner well-being that serves as a thermostat to the outer world, and a happiness built on God's steadfast love. Joy sometimes giggles; sometimes it sighs. Joy does not always belly laugh, but it always bears a knowing smile. Joy is one of the ways God loves us. We can feel His happiness holding us even through the deepest mourning. We choose to receive and express the joy God gives us by rejoicing.

"Always be full of joy in the Lord. I say it again—rejoice!" (Philippians 4:4 NLT). That's what Paul wrote to the Philippian church. And He didn't pen those lofty words from a pleasure cruise; he wrote them from prison. In his letter, he told them that people had disappointed him, but he was still rejoicing. He explained that his plans hadn't turned out as he had hoped, and he was all alone, but he wouldn't stop rejoicing. He shared how he had lost most of his possessions, but he didn't lose any joy. He described how he found himself in hard circumstances, yet he still had joy.

You have that joy too when you have Jesus. People will fail you. Circumstances will be hard, and plans will change, but your joy is not dependent on what you go through; it is determined by who loves you! *God* loves you—deeply—and He expresses that love by giving you His joy. Join in with the joyful Psalmist and sing:

> *You have turned my mourning into joyful dancing.*
> *You have taken away my clothes of mourning and*
> *clothed me with joy. (Psalm 30:11 NLT)*

Ask God today to ignite His "joy unspeakable and full of glory" (1 Peter 1:8 KJV), and then let it loose! Just rejoice no matter what! "Whatever happens, my dear brothers and sisters, rejoice in the Lord" (Philippians 3:1 NLT).

In Colossians
God Completes Me

G od doesn't do anything halfway. He loves you too much to leave you lacking in this life. So when you give your heart to Him, He gives you Himself completely and makes you "complete in Him, who is the head of all principality and power" (Colossians 2:10 NKJV).

Sometimes we feel that nagging fear that something is missing in us, in our experience, or in our efforts. The Christians in Colossae felt the same tug, so Paul wrote them "so that they may have the full riches of complete understanding" about who Jesus is and how He made them right with God" (2:2).

The Colossians were being told they needed more than just Jesus. They were being bombarded with "hollow and deceptive philosophy, which depends on human tradition and the elemental spiritual forces of this world rather than on Christ" (2:8), and they were confused and concerned.

We can feel the way they did because we also

hear about all sorts of good things that we can do or add or think, and it can make us wonder if some extra doing, adding, or thinking will somehow complete our faith experience and make us whole. But God's perfect gift of love, Jesus, has already made you whole. You don't need legalism, philosophy, or mysticism to complete your spiritual experience. You don't need extraordinary wisdom or secret knowledge to make you complete because God made you complete in Christ, "in whom are hidden all the treasures of wisdom and knowledge" (2:3).

When you received Christ, God made you whole. Just as a healthy man doesn't need medicine, you don't need anything else to make you whole either. In this life, if you only have Jesus and nothing else, you lack nothing—you are filled, fulfilled, and complete.

When Jesus died on the cross, He saw you and He loved you. With you on His mind, His final words were, "It is finished." And when He said it, He meant it—it is finished. Completed. Done. Nothing to add. "So then, just as you received Christ Jesus as Lord, continue to live your lives in him" (2:6). Depend on Jesus completely, and experience the completeness He brings.

In 1 Thessalonians
God Returns
to Bring Me
Home with Him

Aday is coming. A remarkable day. A day when God the Father leans toward God the Son and whispers in His ear, *"It's time to get Your bride."* It's the day Jesus, the Lover of your soul, splits the sky wide open and comes down to scoop you up in the clouds to bring you home. "For the Lord himself will come down from heaven with a commanding shout, with the voice of the archangel, and with the trumpet call of God. First, the believers who have died will rise from their graves. Then, together with them, we who are still alive and remain on the earth will be caught up in the clouds to meet the Lord in the air. Then we will be with the Lord forever" (1 Thessalonians 4:16–17 NLT).

Jesus first came as an infant, held in Mary's arms. But one day He will return, and this time He will hold you in His arms forever. *Forever.*

Jesus Himself gave us the promise: "And if I go and prepare a place for you, I will come back and take you to be with me that you also may be where I am" (John 14:3).

Some days you may look to the sky and wish it were "the" day. You may long for the day to come quickly. Sometimes we feel that ache not just because we long to be with Jesus but because we want to be rescued from the sorrow, stress, and pain we can't escape here on earth.

If you feel the longing for "that day," take comfort that "the one who calls you is faithful, and he will do it" (1 Thessalonians 5:24). He will come back for you.

Jesus will return for you because you are His—His beloved child. Trust that until He carries you home with Him, He will carry you through every day of your life. So, "since we belong to the day, let us be sober, putting on faith and love as a breastplate, and the hope of salvation as a helmet" (5:8).

In 2 Thessalonians
God Stands with Me
When I'm Persecuted

God loves us with a powerful love that will not let us down and will not let us go. But His love still lets us suffer, and that's what the Thessalonian Christians were dealing with. So Paul again wrote a letter, and this time he told the weary believers that he was boasting about them to all the other churches, "about your perseverance and faith in all the persecutions and trials you are enduring" (2 Thessalonians 1:4).

The believers in Thessalonica were suffering persecution but standing in faith. The persecution wasn't evidence that they weren't important to God or something was wrong; rather, "all this is evidence that God's judgment is right, and as a result you will be counted worthy of the kingdom of God, for which you are suffering" (1:5).

It is a severe kind of love we feel when God allows the sting of sorrow or the pain of persecution to prove that He sees us as worthy. Yet sometimes that is what love does. It allows us to

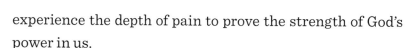

experience the depth of pain to prove the strength of God's power in us.

But when trials or persecutions break our hearts, God has our backs. He was with the believers in Thessalonica, and He is with us too. Know that "in his justice he will pay back those who persecute you" (1:6 NLT).

God doesn't operate with an "us versus them" kind of love. But He does watch out for those who love Him, and He cares for them like a perfect Father, who won't ignore it when His children are mistreated. In "due time" He will make all things right for His children who have been wronged.

Look at the difficulties you face today, and ask God to help you see them through "a full understanding and expression of the love of God" (2 Thessalonians 3:5 NLT), and then give Him your heart because He has your back.

In 1 Timothy
God Entrusts Me
with a High Calling

Thirty years had come and gone since Jesus' death and resurrection. Churches were sprouting up all over the Roman world. The apostle Paul went from town to town like a master gardener, tilling the soil of people's hearts and planting the truth of the gospel deeply in their lives. As a result, churches were growing, and now Paul needed to trust and train others to water that garden. So Paul called on Timothy, his "true son in the faith," a Greek young man Paul had mentored.

God had given Timothy a high calling, and Paul was offering him a letter full of encouragement on how to live out that high calling: "Do not neglect your gift," he told him (1 Timothy 4:14).

God entrusts you with a high calling too, that of loving and leading others as you have been loved and led. Because He loves you, He lifts you up to walk in His ways. And He gives you all the encouragement you need so "that all believers would be filled with love that comes from a pure heart, a clear conscience, and genuine faith" (1:5 NLT).

With a high calling often comes a heavy burden. But Paul told Timothy that it was "Christ . . . who has given me strength to do his work. He considered me trustworthy and appointed me to serve him" (1:12 NLT).

It's a high calling to open your life to God and have His life and love poured into you. Because God values your life, He gives His life to you so you can give His life to others. Just as Paul mentored Timothy and led him to live out his high calling, you, too, have the high calling of loving God and leading another to do the same.

In 2 Timothy
God Gives Me
the Spirit of Power

Sometimes fear feels like Mount Everest! It's like a towering, immovable mountain that overwhelms us and even paralyzes us when we think of overcoming it. It seems bigger than our faith at times. The mountain can appear so looming and large that we are convinced we will never get over it.

Fear is a powerful emotion that can make us feel weak, insecure, and out of control. It can take us off guard and convince us that God doesn't love us or won't help us. But God's love is bigger than every mountain, and His power will make you prevail.

That was the message Paul wanted his young friend Timothy to hear loud and clear. No matter what you face, God's Spirit offers strength to deal with the fears that rise up before you, "for God has not given us a spirit of fear and timidity, but of power, love, and self-discipline" (2 Timothy 1:7 NLT).

The God who loves you gives you power, love, and self-control. That's why you can face your mountain, fortified with the courage to shrink it down to size. God's power gives muscle to your courage.

God's power in you—not your own—gives you the ability to stare down your mountain and "be strong through the grace that God gives you in Christ" (2:1 NLT). God's love motivates your courage. It is His unfailing, unconditional love for you that makes you brave. His "perfect love casts out [all] fear" (1 John 4:18 NKJV).

And God's Spirit will help you maintain courage. The Holy Spirit gives you the sound mind and self-control you need to take "captive every thought to make it obedient to Christ" (2 Corinthians 10:5). That includes fear.

Fear may make you tremble, but God's love makes you triumph! If you are facing a mountain today, don't face it alone. Receive the power, love, and self-control that God offers you. And as you face your fear in His presence, you will be able to say, like the Psalmist, "The mountains melt[ed] like wax at the presence of the LORD" (Psalm 97:5 NKJV).

In Titus God
Steps Into My
Confusion with a
Love That Saves Me

Where would we be if Jesus had not come for us? "Once we, too, were foolish and disobedient. We were misled and became slaves to many lusts and pleasures. Our lives were full of evil and envy, and we hated each other" (Titus 3:3 NLT). Foolish? Misled? Stuck? Evil, envious, and hateful? Not a picture of a peaceful, composed life. But it is a picture of our lives without the love of God.

"But—when God our Savior revealed his kindness and love, he saved us, not because of the righteous things we had done, but because of his mercy. He washed away our sins, giving us a new birth and new life through the Holy Spirit. He generously poured out the Spirit upon us through Jesus Christ our Savior" (3:4–6 NLT). God chose to step into our lives with kindness instead of judgment and with love in place of the rejection we would have shown. He cleaned us up, gave us a new identity, and even shared His Spirit with us. Everything we deserved, God withheld. Everything that should have been out of our reach, love freely extended to us. "Because of his grace he declared us right in his sight and gave us confidence that we will inherit eternal life" (3:7 NLT). God's love interrupts our confusion with clarity and gives us confidence that we are His.

Without Jesus, we would be stuck in darkness and think it was light. We would perpetually settle for less and assume it was as good as it would get. But God's love stepped into history, and His footsteps of peace, purpose, and forgiveness have reverberated through every heart, every nation, and every culture since. Because He came, our confusion is turned to clarity, and foolishness is transformed into faith. Because Love stepped in, humanitarianism has overcome hatred, and envy is replaced with encouraging others.

Take a moment today to think about what your life would be like without the love of God, and thank Him for His grace "that offers salvation to all people" (2:11).

In Philemon
God Turns My
Slavery into
Brotherhood

Onesimus was a slave—no rights, no liberty, no status. One day, when his master, Philemon, wasn't looking, Onesimus robbed him and then ran away. He fled to Rome to find freedom.

But in Rome, he ran into the apostle Paul, who helped him find ultimate freedom—Onesimus found faith in Christ! When Paul met Onesimus, he didn't see a runaway slave; he saw a man God loved, and so he told him about the Messiah.

Though Onesimus became a believer in Jesus the Messiah, he was still a slave. This was AD 60, and Onesimus was the property of Philemon. And he needed to go back. So while Paul was in Rome, he wrote to Philemon to help smooth the way for Onesimus's return: "It seems you lost Onesimus for a little while so that you could have him back forever. He is no longer like a slave to you. He is more than a slave, for he is a beloved brother, especially to me. Now he will mean much more

to you, both as a man and as a brother in the Lord" (Philemon vv. 15–16 NLT).

Philemon could have punished his runaway slave—both the Roman and the Old Testament law gave him that right. But the law of love through the Lord Jesus dictated something better, higher, and far more beautiful: brotherhood. Master and slave could fellowship with each other as brothers.

We too, like Onesimus, once had no rights, no liberty, and no status. We were slaves to sin and defeat. But then we met the Messiah, and our slavery was turned to brotherhood too. We have been given the "right" to be called the sons of God, given liberty from the slavery of sin, and given status as a dearly loved child of God. Look today to the beautiful Master of your soul's salvation, Jesus, and thank Him for turning your slavery into brotherhood. For, "both the one who makes people holy and those who are made holy are of the same family. So Jesus is not ashamed to call them brothers and sisters" (Hebrews 2:11).

In Hebrews
God Invites Me
to Come Boldly
Before His Throne

The door is unlocked for you; it's been thrown wide open! You can come as often as you want, and you can come as you are. You don't need an appointment to the throne room; "all access" is written on your invitation! That's what love does; it welcomes you and invites you in. "Let us therefore come boldly to the throne of grace, that we may obtain mercy and find grace to help in time of need" (Hebrews 4:16 NKJV).

The King of the universe is the God who loves you and invites you to stand before His throne of grace. He loves you so much that He invites you to crawl up into the lap of your Abba Father. When you need it most, He gives you grace.

Before Jesus came, the only way to get to God was through the priests. By making the necessary offerings, the priests, in effect, opened the door between the worshipper and God. But then Jesus became our High Priest! "Seeing then that we have a great High Priest who has passed through the heavens, Jesus the Son of God, let us hold fast our confession. For we do not have a High Priest who cannot sympathize with our weaknesses, but was in all points tempted as we are, yet without sin" (4:14–15 NKJV).

Jesus, our perfect High Priest, has made a way for us to come to God by becoming the perfect offering for us. He is the door we can run through to come to God (John 10:9 NKJV).

Beloved, you don't have to tiptoe or tremble. You don't have to wonder if you are good enough to be there, because you don't have to be. Jesus is. In Christ, you are just as welcome as God's only begotten son. The King of kings is your Father. You are welcome to talk to Him, sit with Him. If you need some grace today, come to His throne. If you need mercy or help, walk through the "door," Jesus Himself, to your Father God and receive everything you need.

In James
God Refines
My Faith

For a piece of silver to become truly magnificent, it must endure extreme heat. When refining silver, the smith carefully holds the precious metal in the fire, where the flames are hottest, so all the impurities are burned away, and nothing remains but radiance.

God's love often holds us in such hot spots: "He . . . sit[s] as a refiner and purifier of silver" (Malachi 3:3). And He does it so that our faith will be refined. God, like a master silversmith, sees our incredible worth and mercifully chooses to let us endure the fire of trials because it reduces impurities, refines us, and brings out our true radiance.

Living through the persecution of Jesus, and the early years of the church, James knew the fire of persecution and trials. He knew how it hurts, but he also knew what it could accomplish. So James said, "Consider it pure joy, my brothers and sisters, whenever you face trials of many

kinds, because you know that the testing of your faith produces perseverance." This refining of our faith makes us "mature and complete, not lacking anything" (James 1:2–4).

God doesn't let you go through hard times and struggles to tear you down but rather to turn you into something remarkable. Trials aren't supposed to define you; God wants trials to refine you.

Though the refining process is never easy, God has you in His hand the whole time you feel the fire. The greater the pressure you feel, the more grace you will experience and the more glory will be revealed in you. For God gives grace generously. As the Scriptures say, "God opposes the proud but gives grace to the humble" (4:6 NLT).

Humbly remain in God's hands, and don't resist that which refines you. God is creating you to be a radiant vessel of honor who reflects the character of Christ.

If today you are feeling the heat of the fire, remember that your loving God is holding you and keeping his eye on you until, like the silversmith in his silver, God sees His image—His beautiful, radiant image—reflected in you.

In 1 Peter
God Gives Me
Victory in Suffering

Faith in Christ doesn't prevent suffering; sometimes it invites it. That's why Peter, the pastor, wrote his letter to the Christians who needed a place to "cast their cares" and be reminded that victory was theirs (1 Peter 5:7 KJV). Twenty years earlier, Stephen, a man full of the Holy Spirit, faced a group of men full of hate. He was stoned to death. The great persecution of Christians had begun (Acts 8:1). The followers of Jesus ran for their lives. They dispersed throughout all Roman provinces, but they didn't outrun what Stephen endured; persecution and suffering found them.

Persecution and suffering always seem to find us too—we can't outrun them or hide either. From the days of the early apostles all the way to today, believers have faced pressure ranging from minor discrimination to murderous rage. We may not know what kind of suffering we will get in this life, but we do know that because we are loved by God, He gives us victory in our suffering. When you are insulted or isolated or ignored because of your faith, you have victory because "the Spirit of glory and of God rests on you" (1 Peter 4:14).

When you face devastating loss, you still have victory because you have a "priceless inheritance—an inheritance that is kept in heaven for you, pure and undefiled, beyond the reach of change and decay" (1:4 NLT). And ultimately, when you face death, you have victory because you have "a living hope through the resurrection of Jesus Christ from the dead" (1:3).

God's love doesn't always keep suffering from us, but His love keeps suffering from destroying us. So if you feel pressure or persecution today because of your faith in Christ, cast all your anxiety on the God who loves you, because He really does care (5:7). Ask God today to remind you that you don't fight for a position of victory; you fight from a position of victory because of Christ. "For Christ also suffered once for sins, the righteous for the unrighteous, to bring you to God" (3:18).

In 2 Peter
God Gives Me
Everything I
Need for Life
and Godliness

Do you ever imagine what your life would be like if you had an unlimited supply of money? What if you could buy everything you want? If you had everything you *want* in this life, though, would you have everything you *need*?

Because God loves you, He gives you all you need for this life—and it's far more valuable than an unlimited supply of dollars. "By his divine power, God has given us everything we need for living a godly life. We have received all of this by coming to know him, the one who called us to himself by means of his marvelous glory and excellence" (2 Peter 1:3 NLT).

Sometimes we only see what we lack, what we wish we had, or how much better our lives would be if we just had that one more thing—that better job or higher salary or lower debt, or bigger house or newer car or a few more dollars in the bank. But everything you need for living a fulfilling life, you've already got in Jesus! When you know

Jesus, you lack nothing and have been given everything you need! As you spend your life growing in the knowledge of God, it leads to "grace and peace" being "multiplied" in your life! (1:2 NKJV). And as grace and peace are multiplied in your life, your contentment grows, and godliness increases.

The God who loves you would never leave you without everything you need in this life. He has given you what you need most; He has given you His Son, Jesus, and in giving you Jesus, He has given you life. "In him was life, and that life was the light of all mankind" (John 1:4). Look today to Jesus and draw your life from Him. To know Jesus is to have everything you need. Tap into the currency of His limitless love today and experience the contentment you long for.

In 1 John
God Makes
Me Clean

Everybody sins. Every person since the dawn of time has blown it and come up short compared to God's perfection. Adam and Eve started it, and everyone—from the most devout to the most depraved among us—has kept it up ever since. It's our nature to sin. "If we claim to be without sin, we deceive ourselves and the truth is not in us" (1 John 1:8). But it is the loving nature of God to forgive sin and cleanse us! God takes our sin and makes us brand-new through "the blood of Jesus, his Son," and, no matter what we've done, He "purifies us from all sin" (1:7).

If you feel as though your soul is dirty and your spirit is weighed down by layers and layers of guilt from sin, God's love is waiting with the forgiveness you crave. Just tell God. Admit your sin and ask Him to clean you up. He will: "If we confess our sins, he is faithful and just and will forgive us our sins and purify us from all unrighteousness" (1:9).

Love doesn't overlook the sin that hurts us and dishonors God. Love points out our sins so we can confess them and then makes a way to erase them. The God who loves you forgives you when you ask Him to. He washes you clean and gives you a fresh start. Your sin is lost in the shadow of His forgiveness, covered by the royal train of His mercy and majesty. That's what God does. The prophet Micah cried, "You will tread our sins underfoot and hurl all our iniquities into the depths of the sea" (Micah 7:19).

He doesn't forgive us because we deserve it; He forgives us because in His mercy He decided to. When God makes you clean, you radiate His beauty, and when He looks at you, He only sees the radiance of Jesus' pure and righteous life. He no longer sees your sin. So receive and feel the love of God today by confessing your sin and being cleansed by His forgiveness. Then you can humbly say, "For You have cast all my sins behind Your back" (Isaiah 38:17 NKJV). And when it comes to your forgiven sin, God does not have eyes in the back of His head!

In 2 John
God Shows Me
How to Finish Well

It's often a lot easier to start something than to finish it. We get road weary, distracted by detours, and often we get just plain worn out and want to quit. But God's love helps us stand firm and stay strong.

The apostle John knew that so well. As an old man, he picked up his pen with his wrinkled hand and wrote to "the chosen lady and her children, whom I love in truth; and not only I, but also all who know the truth" (2 John v. 1 NASB), to instruct and encourage them to hang in there and stay faithful. He called himself "the elder," and he may have actually been writing to an upstanding woman and her children, but more likely he was writing to a persecuted church and was using "chosen lady" as a code to help protect them. Either way the truths in the thirteen verses of John's second letter are for us and remind us how God loves us. He loves us enough to boost us when the race is long and the finish line feels far

away. What you started with faith, you can complete with faithfulness because God shows you how to finish well.

You can finish well because of the truth, "which lives in us and will be with us forever" (v. 2).

You can finish well because you "walk in obedience to his commands. As you have heard from the beginning, his command is that you walk in love" (v. 6).

You can finish well because God carries you when you're weary, carries on what He started, and carries the weight of the world when you feel you may crumble beneath it.

The hardest things you face usually turn out to be the best things. So don't miss out because you give up or give in. Keep walking by faith, because you will one day walk across that finish line. Until then, thank God, for "grace, mercy and peace from God the Father and from Jesus Christ, the Father's Son, will be with us in truth and love" (v. 3).

In 3 John
God Offers
Me Hospitality
When I Need
a Place to Rest

Sometimes heaviness of heart and soul makes us feel weary and worn-out. We need time and a place where we can rest our souls. Jesus understands that weariness; He felt it. He and many of His followers were traveling preachers without a home of their own. They didn't have a place to just rest. But God's love through God's people became that resting place. They showed "care for the traveling teachers who pass through," and they offered "loving friendship" even though many were strangers (3 John vv. 5–6 NLT).

God's love is our resting place. He shows care for each of us as we're traveling through the ups and downs of this life. He opens His heart to us when we need a place to call home. He offers unconditional hospitality to us even when we carry old, heavy baggage. God's love for you is a safe place where you are always welcome—more than welcome, you are wanted and waited for. God longs to shelter you.

This I declare about the L̲ᴏ̲ʀᴅ:
He alone is my refuge, my place of safety;
*   he is my God, and I trust him. (Psalm 91:2 ɴʟᴛ)*

If you are road-weary today because your journey is long and hard, come on in and settle into God's love for you. You can rest in His hospitality. Just as Jesus welcomed the little children to come to Him, He welcomes you to come to Him so He can take you in His arms, place "His hands on" you, and bless you (Matthew 19:13–15). His love will tuck you in and whisper His peace over you as you rest securely in His grace and generosity.

Receive God's generous invitation to rest in Him, and then share His love and hospitality today with someone who may need a safe place to rest. As the Bible says, "Do not forget to show hospitality to strangers, for by so doing some people have shown hospitality to angels without knowing it" (Hebrews 13:2).

In Jude God
Keeps Me from
Falling and Presents
Me Faultless Before
His Throne

The love that drew your heart to Christ is the same love that will deliver you to heaven someday. And along the way, God's love will keep you from falling—He will hold you together so you don't fall apart, and He'll hold you close so you won't fall away. That's what love does—it holds you up and keeps you from falling even when you stumble.

Maybe Jude had stumbled some in his life. He was Jesus' half brother, but he didn't become a believer in Christ until after Jesus' resurrection. But once he believed, he assured us that we are kept, we are held, "by God the Father, who loves you and keeps you safe in the care of Jesus Christ" (Jude v. 1 NLT).

Even if you stumble, God's love won't let you fall away. When life trips you up, you may fall, but you will just fall deeper into His unfailing grace and forgiveness.

You are held in the safety, security, and love

of God. You may falter now and then, but because God's love keeps you, you will never fall so far that God will not pull you back to His forgiving heart. He holds you and keeps you to "present you before his glorious presence without fault and with great joy" (v. 24). Eventually, all your faltering will be lost in God's forgiveness, and the result will be a shimmering, sparkling presentation of God's grace.

God will one day present you before His own throne, once flawed yet now faultless. Like a brilliant diamond with perfect clarity, you will stand before God, beaming, blameless, and beautiful, because it will be Jesus' character that shines in you. He will carry you every day of your life. He protects you so He can present you to the Father. Thank Him for His forgiveness and for keeping you close to Him. With such a beautiful Savior and loving Father, offer your deepest gratitude today. "To the only God our Savior be glory, majesty, power and authority, through Jesus Christ our Lord, before all ages, now and forevermore! Amen" (v. 25).

In Revelation
God Receives Me
as His Beloved and
Treasured Bride

The guests have been seated. The candles are lit. The attendants have walked down the aisle, brilliantly colored bouquets in hand. The music swells. The minister signals for everyone to stand. Every eye is focused . . . but not on the bride. Every eye turns to the One and Only: the Groom, the main character of this love story. The apostle John described Him this way: "I saw heaven standing open and there before me was a white horse, whose rider is called Faithful and True. . . . On his head are many crowns" (Revelation 19:11–12).

This marriage celebration is like none other. It centers on the unveiling of Jesus, the Lamb of God, your Savior, the One and only King of the universe. All eyes are fixed on the Beautiful One as the magnificent choir sings:

"Hallelujah!
For our Lord God Almighty reigns.

Let us rejoice and be glad
   and give him glory!
For the wedding of the Lamb has come,
   and his bride has made herself ready." (19:6–7)

The bride beholds the Groom. She is finally there. You are there. God's beloved people, His church, are His bride. And God Himself has made the bride ready. He has purified His church and made us holy. He dresses us in a radiant garment of "fine linen, bright and clean" (19:8).

The joy we will feel over such an undeserved union will be felt by Jesus too. Jesus Christ, the Bridegroom, will beam with joy and pride when we, His restored children, His redeemed church, are by His side forever.

God has poured out His love on us—not just sixty-six ways—a million ways. But nothing compares to the way we will experience His love at the wedding feast of the Lamb, when we will behold our Bridegroom. He's coming for us—He's coming for you, His beloved and treasured bride. "He who testifies to these things says, 'Yes, I am coming soon.'" And you and I say, today and every day, "Amen. Come, Lord Jesus" (22:20).